FOLENS IDEAS BANK SONGS AND RHYMES

Ian Sharp

Contents

How to use this book	2	Rhymes in music	26
Introduction	3	Pitch ideas – two notes	28
There was a princess long ago	4	Pitch ideas – three notes	30
Pease pudding hot	6	High and low	32
Hot cross buns	8	More sets of notes	34
One, two, three, four, five	10	Sailing and playing	36
Chiming clocks	12	Forest music	38
Singing and clapping games	14	Lullaby baby	40
More singing games	16	Marching along	42
What's in a name?	18	Contrasts	44
Rhymes, games and chants	20	Old and new	46
Rap in the kitchen	22	Musical glossary	48
Keeping time!	24		

How to use this book

Ideas Bank books provide ready to use, practical, photocopiable activity pages for children, **plus** a wealth of ideas for extension and development.

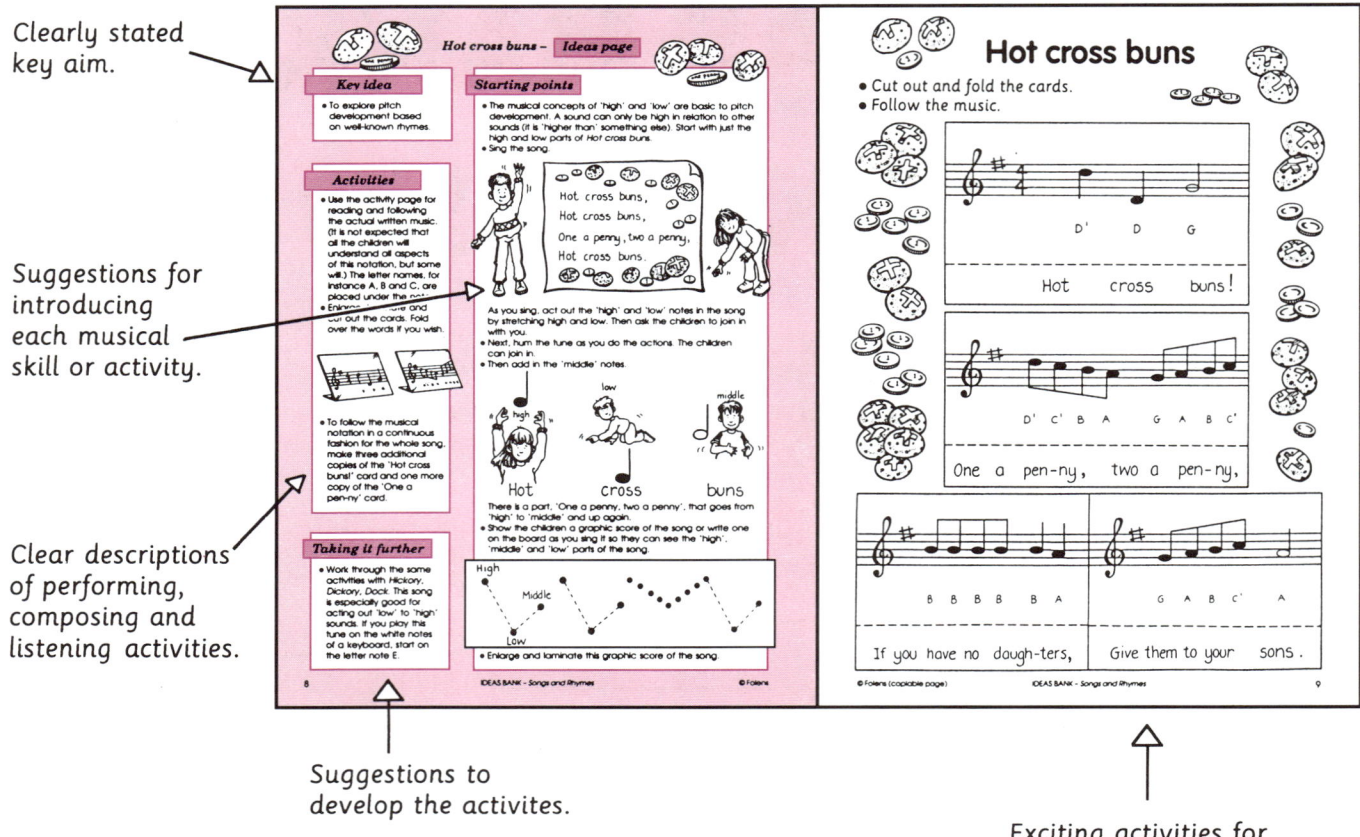

- Clearly stated key aim.
- Suggestions for introducing each musical skill or activity.
- Clear descriptions of performing, composing and listening activities.
- Suggestions to develop the activites.
- Exciting activities for independent or group work.

Folens allows photocopying of pages marked 'copiable page' for educational use, providing that this use is within the confines of the purchasing institution. Copiable pages should not be declared in any return in respect of any photocopying licence.

Folens books are protected by international copyright laws. All rights are reserved. The copyright of all materials in this book, except where otherwise stated, remains the property of the publisher and author(s). No part of this publication may be reproduced, stored in a retrieval system, or transmitted, in any form or by any means, for whatever purpose, without the written permission of Folens Limited.

This resource may be used in a variety of ways. However, it is not intended that teachers or children should write directly into the book itself. Ian Sharp hereby assert his moral rights to be identified as the author of this work in accordance with the Copyright, Designs and Patents Act 1988.

Editor: Alyson Jones
Illustrations and cover image: Susan Hutchison – Graham-Cameron Illustration

Layout artist: Patricia Hollingsworth
Cover design: In Touch Creative Services

© 1996 Folens Limited, on behalf of the author(s).

Every effort has been made to contact copyright holders of material used in this book. If any have been overlooked, we will be pleased to make any necessary arrangements.

British Library Cataloguing in Publication Data. A catalogue record for this book is available from the British Library.

First published 1996 by Folens Limited, Dunstable and Dublin.

Folens Limited, Albert House, Apex Business Centre, Boscombe Road, Dunstable, LU5 4RL, England.

ISBN 1 85276884-3

Printed in Singapore by Craft Print.

Introduction

Songs and rhymes, the traditional games and music of a child's early years, are at the heart of musical development. Some children already have a rich background of music that is developed at home or in a playgroup before they come to school. Children can learn so much from singing, chanting, playing and listening, as every class teacher of young children knows. Through the songs and rhymes of childhood, children can develop the skills, interest and attitudes that will stay with them throughout their school days and beyond.

The practical classroom projects in this book are linked to photocopiable activities. These also tie in with National Curriculum objectives for Music through the two attainment targets – 'performing and composing' and 'listening and appraising'. The ideas could be used on their own or in conjunction with other published schemes. They range from reception to year 2 and could be adapted for the needs of individual children or groups.

The organisation of teaching activities in this book will vary. In general, the material is best introduced as a class lesson. Many of the projects are flexible, giving plenty of opportunity for individual approaches. In many cases the activities are intended to support rather than lead practical and creative music-making. This book is not designed to be worked through in sequence, it is intended as a 'dip-in' resource. In all cases the teacher is strongly advised to have a well-formulated idea of the possibilities for open-ended and creative work.

When children are familiar with the methods of working and can co-operate over the use of resources, then group activities will quickly follow. Individual work, too, should be encouraged. In this way the music curriculum will differentiate between children of varying abilities. Some children between the ages of five and seven will still find it difficult to maintain a steady pulse (beat) and to read words or musical notation. Other children, though, will be more noticeably sophisticated in their grasp of musical concepts and skills.

Above all, it is making music that is the most important consideration. Theoretical knowledge about music is no substitute for actually taking part in music-making. This is why the 'sing–say–play' approach of *Ideas Bank Songs and Rhymes* should enable teachers and children alike to build on the known and to explore music with confidence, enjoyment and personal satisfaction.

There was a princess long ago – Ideas page

Key ideas

- To make a musical performance based on a traditional song.
- To explore the musical concept of 'high' and 'low' sounds.

Starting points

- Ask the children to sing *There was a princess long ago* and do the actions shown in the illustrations.

There was a princess long ago ...

And she lived in a big high tower.

One day a fairy (bad queen) waved her wand.

The princess slept for a thousand years.

A great big forest grew around.

A gallant prince came riding by.

He cut the trees down with his sword.

He took her hand to wake her up.

So everybody's happy now.

- Add a drum to tap out the basic pulse of the song.

- Then use a different instrument, for instance, a tambourine, to play the rhythm of all the words, one verse at a time.

- Ask the children to choose some instruments that would reflect each character in the story. Remind them that the princess goes to sleep and then wakes up so she will need two different sounds to indicate this change.
- Select some children to play these instruments when each character is mentioned and to accompany the singers. All the children should make 'happy' sounds for the last verse.

Activities

- Enlarge the activity page and cut out the illustrations. Place the princess at the bottom of the castle steps – this is the 'music ladder'. Illustrate this 'low' position by making low pitched sounds on a tuned percussion instrument.
- Place the princess high up in the tower and make a higher pitched sound.
- Then randomly place the princess on the steps or in the tower and ask the children if she is 'high' or 'low'. They should take it in turns to play the tuned instrument to indicate where she is on the steps.

Taking it further

- Ask the children to enact a puppet version of the song. They will need to draw more characters and make them into finger or rod puppets.
- Link with the traditional story of *Sleeping Beauty*, especially at pantomime time.

There was a princess ...

Pease pudding hot – Ideas page

Key idea

- To use rhymes as a rhythm resource.

Activities

- Enlarge, cut out and laminate the cards on the activity page. Place the cards lengthways to make a complete musical score. (The children could help.)
- Fold along the dotted line on each card so that only the rhythm notation is showing. Ask the children to match each rhythm with the correct words. (The words for cards A and B are different, but not the music!)
- Use the 'ostinato' pattern (a pattern that is repeated) on the cards for music reading and playing. For instance, the rhythm of card C is quite distinctive and could fit in with many other songs and instrumental pieces, as an accompaniment pattern.

Starting points

- Sing *Twinkle, twinkle, little star* with the children.
- Ask them to clap or play the basic pulse (beat) as they sing.

  Twin-kle, twin-kle lit-tle star

- Play the rhythm of the words and stop at the end of a line. Ask the question 'Where are we now?'. The children should try to tell you. They will probably need to sing as they play!
- Enlarge the score of the song below to make a poster. Point to the musical notes as the song is sung or played on an instrument such as the claves. The words and the musical notes are spaced out in the 'shape' of the lines of the music. You do not need to explain the crotchet (one beat) or minim (two beats) at this stage, just follow the shape of the music.
- The two boxes of rhythm notation at the bottom of the score can be used for the whole song.

Taking it further

- Arrange a nursery rhyme competition. Divide the children into two teams. Team A starts by singing one verse of a nursery rhyme and then sings *The Alphabet song*.
- Team B, without hesitation, sings a different song, followed again by *The Alphabet song*.
- The game goes on until one team cannot think of a new song and then that team is 'out'.

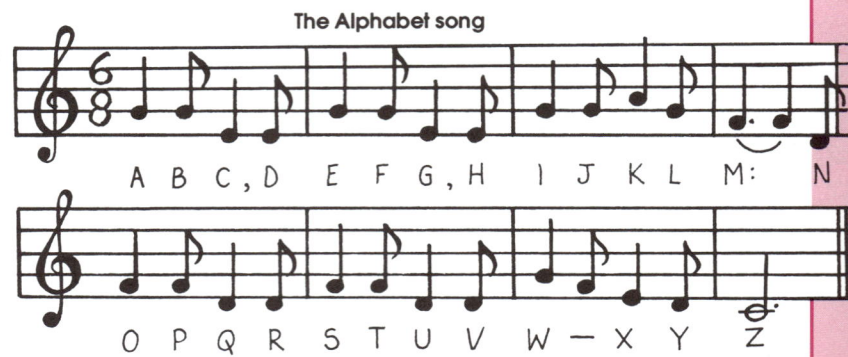

Pease pudding hot

- Cut out and fold each card.
- Can you fit the music to the words?

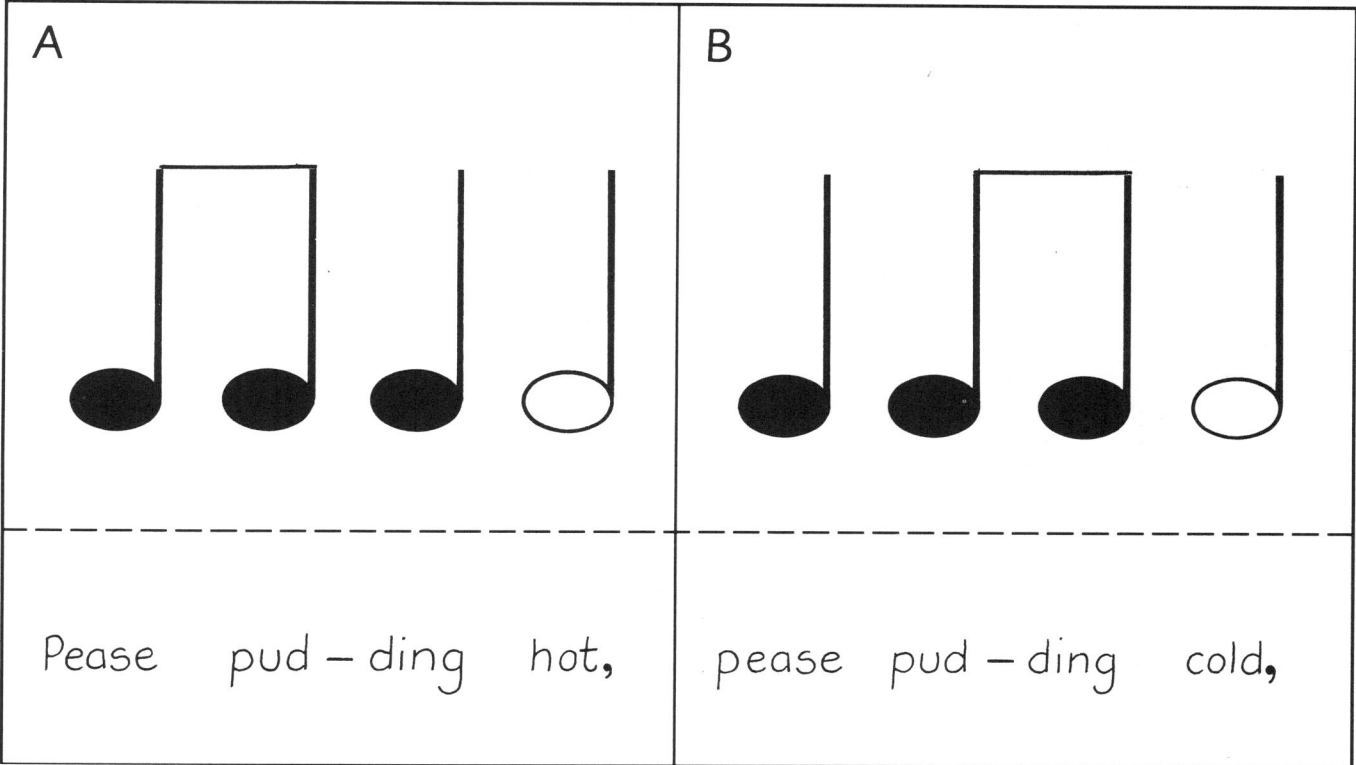

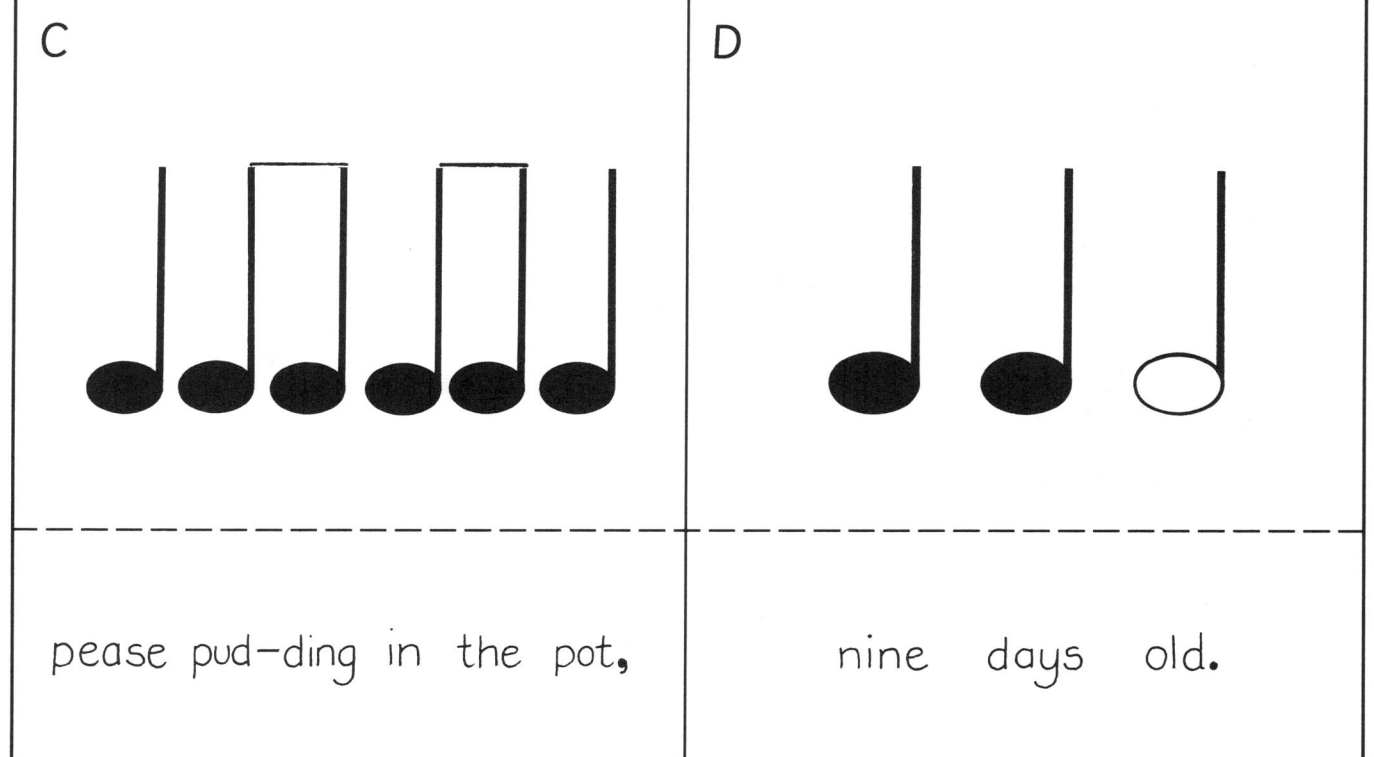

Hot cross buns – Ideas page

Key idea
- To explore pitch development based on well-known rhymes.

Activities
- Use the activity page for reading and following the actual written music. (It is not expected that all the children will understand all aspects of this notation, but some will.) The letter names, for instance A, B and C, are placed under the notes.
- Enlarge, laminate and cut out the cards. Fold over the words if you wish.

- To follow the musical notation in a continuous fashion for the whole song, make three additional copies of the 'Hot cross buns!' card and one more copy of the 'One a pen-ny' card.

Taking it further
- Work through the same activities with *Hickory, Dickory, Dock*. This song is especially good for acting out 'low' to 'high' sounds. If you play this tune on the white notes of a keyboard, start on the letter note E.

Starting points
- The musical concepts of 'high' and 'low' are basic to pitch development. A sound can only be high in relation to other sounds (it is 'higher than' something else). Start with just the high and low parts of *Hot cross buns*.
- Sing the song.

As you sing, act out the 'high' and 'low' notes in the song by stretching high and low. Then ask the children to join in with you.
- Next, hum the tune as you do the actions. The children can join in.
- Then add in the 'middle' notes.

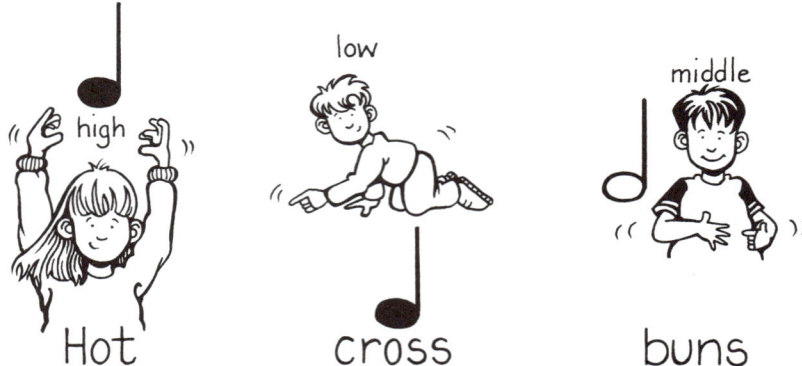

There is a part, 'One a penny, two a penny', that goes from 'high' to 'middle' and up again.
- Show the children a graphic score of the song or write one on the board as you sing it so they can see the 'high', 'middle' and 'low' parts of the song.

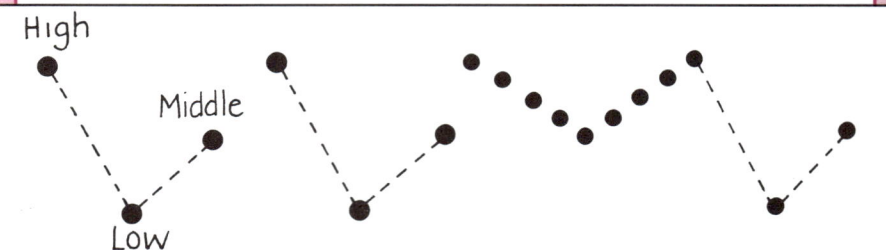

- Enlarge and laminate this graphic score of the song.

8   IDEAS BANK – *Songs and Rhymes*   © Folens

Hot cross buns

- Cut out and fold the cards.
- Follow the music.

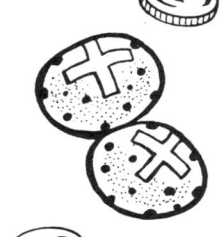

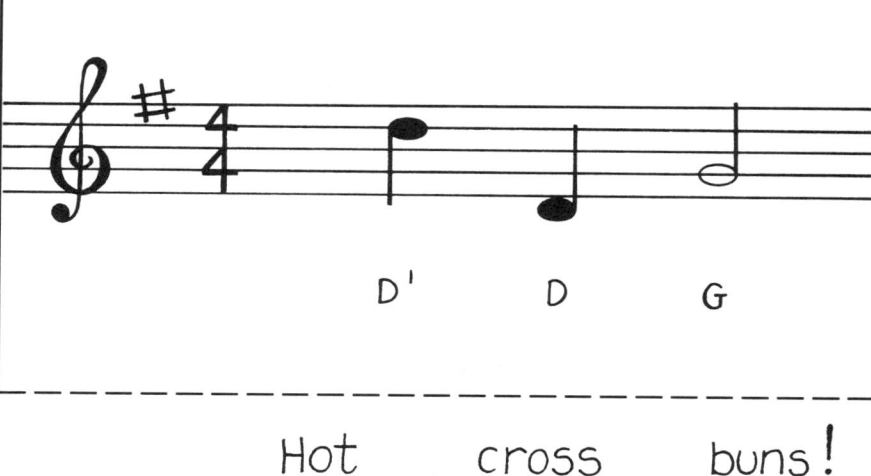

D' D G

Hot   cross   buns!

D' C' B A   G A B C'

One a pen-ny, two a pen-ny,

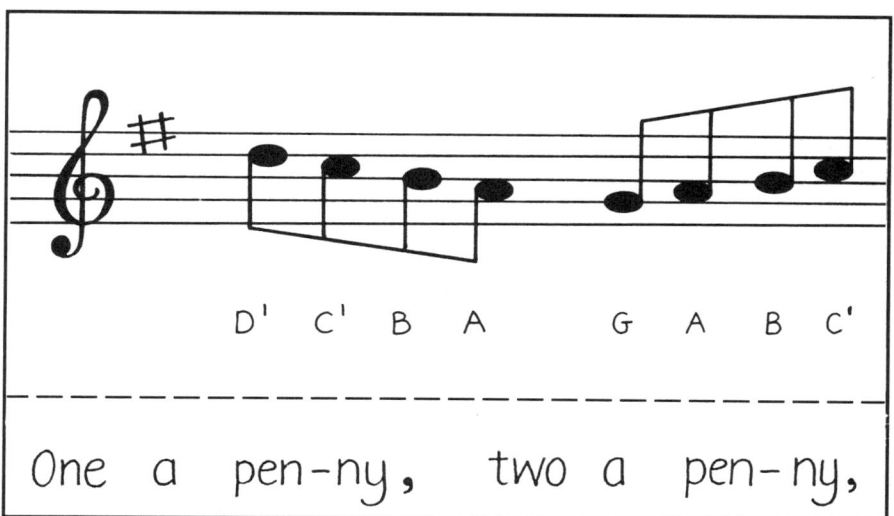

B B B B B A

If you have no daugh-ters,

G A B C' A

Give them to your   sons.

© Folens (copiable page)   IDEAS BANK – *Songs and Rhymes*

12345 One, two, three, four, five – Ideas page

Key idea

- To introduce counting, thinking and playing.

Starting points

- Use different percussion instruments to emphasise the numbers in this song. Have one instrument play when each number is sung and continue the pattern for lines E and G if this repetition is clear to the children.

Taking it further

- Number songs and rhymes have their own numerical and logical pattern that are brought out in music.
- A song with decreasing numbers is *Five currant buns in a baker's shop*. A group of five instruments could play the first verse and then four for the next verse and so on. *Ten green bottles* could be played in the same way.
- Examples of songs with increasing numbers are *Peter hammers with one hammer* and *One man went to mow*.
- If you have enough instruments arrange the children in groups of two or three, or an individual child could play at the appropriate place in the song.
- Alternatively, the children could play the correct number of sounds before each verse. This is harder and should only be suggested if the children can count really well!

Activities

- In Liverpool there was a famous police horse, Stanley, who was able to count. Children would give him a sum and he would tap out the answer with his hoof. How do the children think he did it? (Perhaps someone was helping him!)
- Ask the children to do some sums in musical code. Divide the class into groups of four and give each child a copy of the activity page and an instrument to play (a triangle, a cymbal, a drum and a tambourine). Explain that the number of beats on the triangle represents the numbers they will have to add together.

Individual numbers = 🔺🔺🔺 = ♩ ♩ ♩
                                  1 2 3

A clash of the cymbals means they will have to add these numbers together.

Add = 💥 = !

Two short beats on the drum means they have to take away these numbers.

Take away = 🥁 🥁 = ⊓

The tambourine means 'equals' and should be shaken until they have the answer to the sum.

Equals = 🪘 = ∿∿∿∿∿

The answer should be given as the correct number of beats on the triangle again. (Remember that for many children the concept of 'add' is hard enough.)

- The children should 'play' and complete the musical sums on the activity page and then create some of their own.
- Below are some additional symbols that one child could play on a glockenspiel or xylophone.

multiply (sounds get louder)   divide (sounds get softer)

Chiming clocks – Ideas page

Key idea

- To listen to the sounds made by clocks and to compose some music.

Starting points

- Use the clock face on the activity page to tell the time. Some children may find it difficult to read from a traditional clock face (it may be a new experience for them). Later, you could experiment with Roman figures, but start with Arabic numerals.
- Find a suitable note on a chime bar or glockenspiel for your clock to strike. Set the hands on the clock face and make the clock strike the right time. Then change the time.
- Explain that clocks make different sounds, such as high or low. Cuckoo clocks usually strike two notes. Try a high C and an A for a cuckoo clock effect.

Activities

- The following song can be sung to the Big Ben tune. Explain that some clocks strike the quarter hours. *Westminster Chimes* can be split up into quarters. At quarter past the hour play the first quarter. At half past the hour play the first quarter again followed by the second quarter.

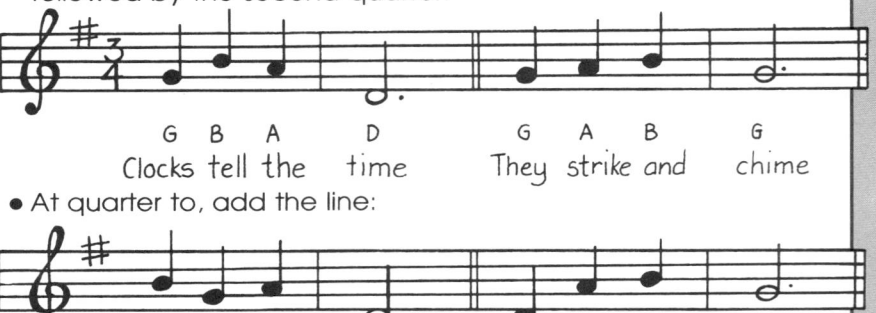

- At quarter to, add the line:

- On the hour sing the whole song, followed by the clock striking the hour.

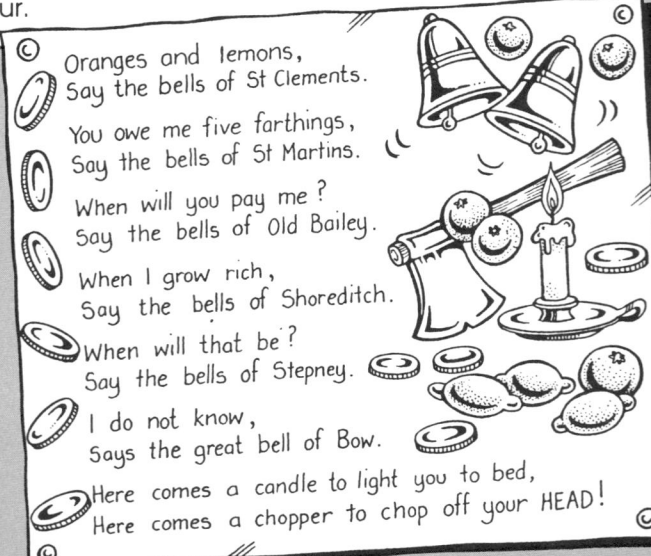

Taking it further

- In a city centre at noon the children might hear several clocks chiming the time. Divide them into groups and sing *Oranges and lemons*. Let them select suitable instruments to make the sounds of each bell chiming.
- Arrange for the bells to strike at six o'clock. Remember that they don't all need to strike at the same time. One clock might be rather slow. Use the clock on the activity page to indicate the time.
- Illustrate with sound effects some songs and stories connected with clocks. For instance in the story of *Cinderella* a clock will strike at midnight and for *Hickory, Dickory, Dock* add the sound of a clock striking at one.

Chiming clocks

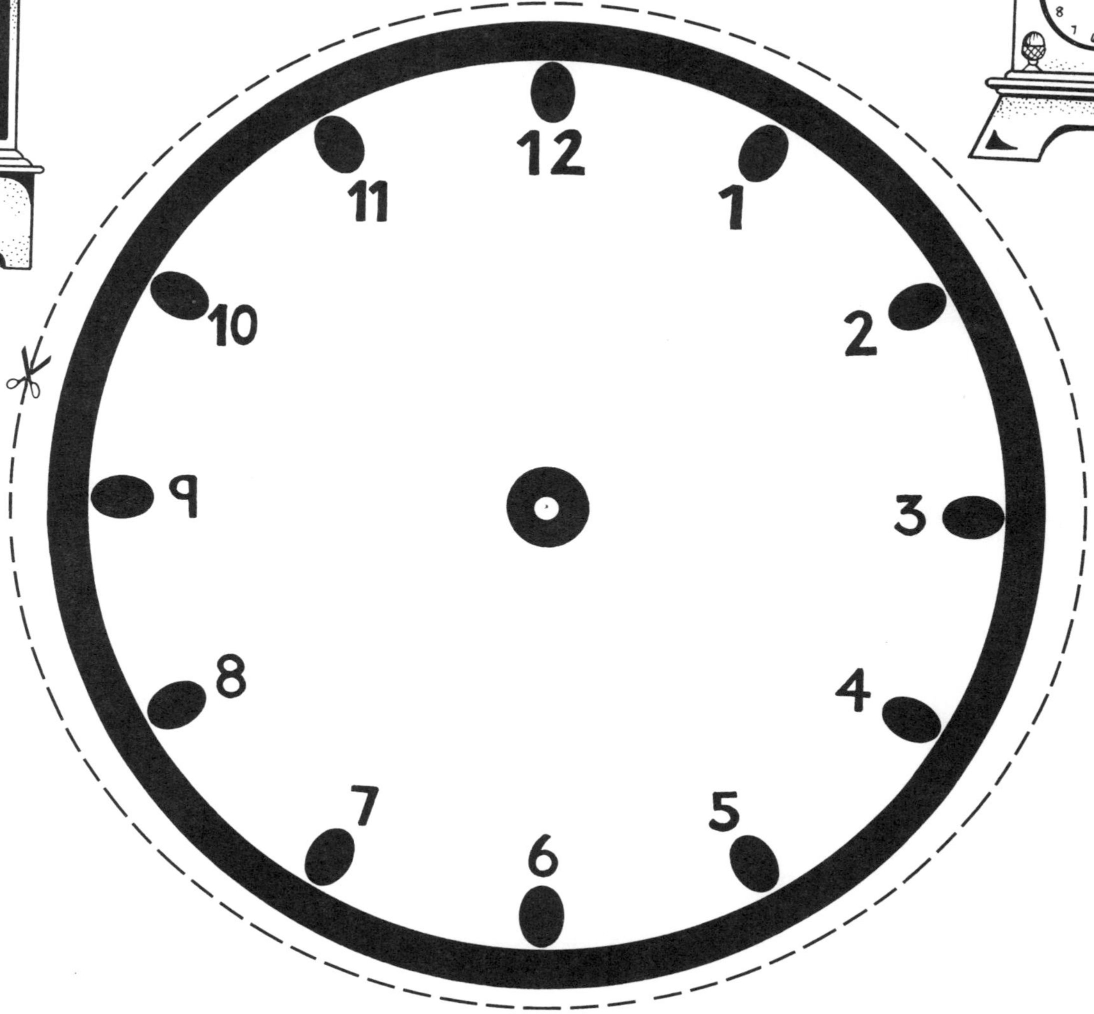

clock face

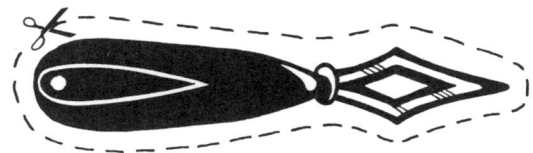

big hand

little hand

Singing and clapping games – Ideas page

Key idea

- To use and appraise traditional singing and clapping games in a performance context.

Activities

- Use the picture on the activity page to make a poster or give each child a copy to colour. The picture is taken from a woodcut dating from 1497 and shows a version of *Oranges and lemons*. Not much seems to have changed in the basic idea of this singing game.
- Discuss the picture with the class. Are the children in the picture playing a game? Draw attention to the two players holding hands to make an arch. This should give the children a clue as to which game is being played. Do they think the picture is based on an older one? How can they tell? Is the game still played today and if so, is it the same?

Here comes a chopper to chop off your head!

Starting points

- Sing and clap this song.

> I went to a Chinese restaurant
> To buy a loaf of bread, bread, bread,
> They wrapped it up in a five pound note
> And this is what they said, said, said:
>
> My name is ...
> O–U–T spells out!

- Sing the words of the traditional Caribbean song, *Dutch girl*.

> I am a pretty little Dutch girl,
> As pretty as pretty can be
> And all the boys around my square
> Go crazy-crazy over me.
>
> My boyfriend's name is Tommy,
> He come from far Ammambo,
> With a big red nose and ten tippy toes
> And that's the way my story goes.
>
> One day he gave me pictures,
> One day he gave me pears,
> One day he gave me fifty cents
> And kicked me down the stairs.
>
> I gave him back his pictures,
> I gave him back his pears,
> I gave him back his fifty cents
> And kicked him down the stairs.

- The children will probably be quick to point out that this Caribbean version of the rhyme is slightly different from theirs. How does their own version go? Can they sing it to you?
- Do the boys and girls in your school play any clapping games? They could make a list of the games they play. Do these change during the course of the year? They could record how to play each game using a tape recorder or video recorder, or by drawing and writing the rules.

Taking it further

- Ask the children to find out if any of their older relatives remember playing any games, such as *When Susie was a baby* and *Wind the bobbin*. How did these games go?
- There could be an opportunity to share games with children from another school or another country. For instance, *Pass the pebble on* is a game from Ghana that is often played today in many schools.

Singing games

- What game is being played?
- Is this game still played today?

More singing games – Ideas page

Key idea

- To use and appraise traditional singing games in a performance context.

Activities

- Traditional games still survive and there are modern versions, such as the *Hokey Cokey*, that are played by adults and children. A modern song, such as *The Birdie song* might well become 'traditional' in time! How many games do the children know? They could make a list.
- Organise a festival of singing games in your class or school. Record the games and produce a Festival Book.
- Some games represent past times. *The Baker* (sung to the tune of *Here we go round the Mulberry bush*) is typical of the late Victorian period. How can the children tell this song is old? They could act out each verse. Why not dress up in Victorian costume!
- Give the children copies of the activity page. It shows line drawings of two games, *Nuts in May* and *Poor Jenny is a-weeping*. (The words for the latter are on page 44.) Can the children guess which game is which? They could give reasons for their choices.

Starting points

- Sing the traditional 'line' game song, *Nuts in May*.

Here we come gathering nuts in May,
Nuts in May, nuts in May.
Here we come gathering nuts in May,
On a cold and frosty morning.

Who will you have for nuts in May? *and so on.*

We'll have (*name*) for nuts in May *and so on.*

Who will you have to pull her away? *and so on.*

We'll have (*name*) to pull her away *and so on.*

- Now sing the 'circle' game song, *Nuts in May*.

Here we go Lubin Loo, here we go Lubin Light,
Here we go Lubin Loo, all on a Saturday night.

You put your right foot in, You put your right foot out,
You shake it a little, a little, And turn yourself about.

You put your left foot in *and so on.*

You put your right hand in *and so on.*

You put your left hand in *and so on.*

You put your noses in *and so on.*

You put your whole selves in *and so on.*

The Baker

This is the way the baker makes
Pies and buns, bread and cakes,
And all the sparks so fast and bright
Run up the oven chimney.

This is the way he carries the bread,
Held so well on the top of his head.
And all the sparks so fast and bright
Run up the oven chimney.

This is the way they chop the wood
To make the oven warm and good.
And all the sparks *and so on.*

This is the way the baker's man
Goes on his rounds as fast as he can.
And all the sparks *and so on.*

This is the way we eat the cakes,
The pies and buns the baker makes.
And all the sparks *and so on.*

Taking it further

- Composers have sometimes used children's games as the starting point for their music. Play extracts from Bizet's *Children's Games* and Bartok's piano pieces, *For Children* and ask the children to guess which games they can hear.

Singing games

- Which games are being played?

What's in a name? – Ideas page

Key idea
- To develop the concept of rhythm.

Activities
- Ask the children to find which of the following names match the rhythm notation on the activity page.

- They could match the sound of other names with the rhythm notation on the activity page.
- Sing or chant a song in which you invite the children to respond by chanting the rhythm of their own names. You could use the *Bye Baby Bunting* tune. (Some children might be shy about this, so be prepared to accept any way in which the name is 'sung' back to the class.)

Starting points
- Every word and name has its own rhythm pattern. Choose a child's name and try saying it several times to establish its sound. It will make a rhythm 'ostinato' pattern. Opposite are some lines from *Disobedience* by A A Milne as an example.
- Then sing the name making either a two-note tune using the notes G and E or a three-note tune using A, G and E. You could try to sing all the names on your school register!
- Put several children's names together and repeat this sequence several times to form a longer chant. For instance,

  Anthony, Adam, Keya, Kim

- As you say or sing the chant, play the rhythm on percussion instruments, such as the claves or bongos. Then play the rhythm as you whisper the words or think the words without saying them. Use this rhythm chant to make part of a longer piece of music.

Disobedience

James James Morrison Morrison
Weatherby George Dupree
Took great care of his mother,
Though he was only three.

James James Morrison Morrison
Commonly known as Jim
Told his other relations
Not to go blaming him.

Taking it further
- Make rhythm cards to match names with one, two or three syllables. Copy and laminate the cards and put two or more cards together to make up longer names if needed.
- Write the children's names on the bottom half of the cards and bend this section over or wipe clean when you need to write in a new name. You must check the number of 'sounding' syllables of each name carefully.

18 IDEAS BANK – *Songs and Rhymes* © Folens

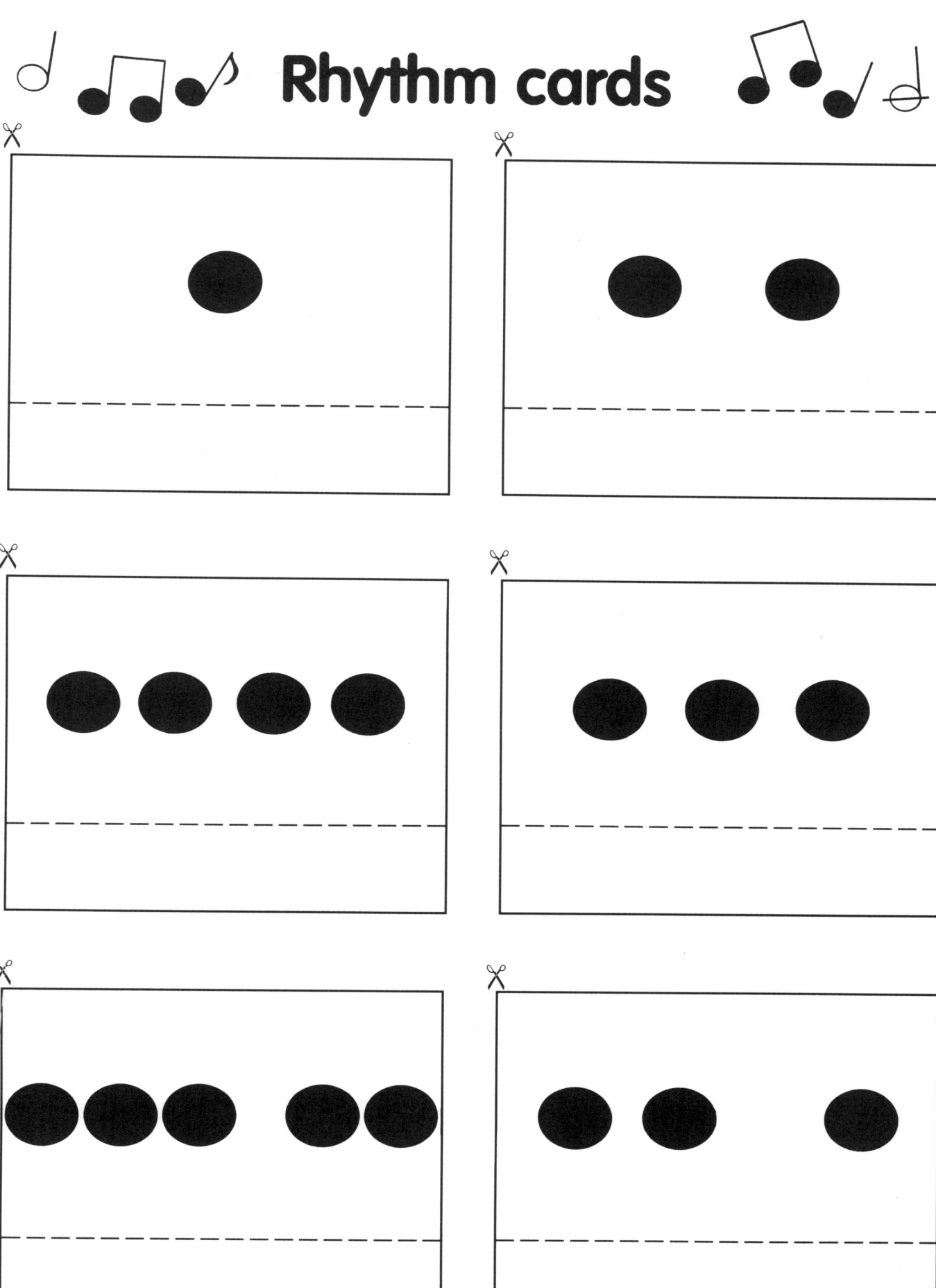

Rhymes, games and chants – Ideas page

Key ideas

- To work with structure and notation in music.
- To make a longer piece of music out of short fragments.

Activities

- Ask the children to cut out and match the notes with the correct words on the activity page. The completed boxes make a rhythm chant.

- Paste the completed boxes on to card. Cut out and fold along the dotted lines so that the words are hidden. Play a section and ask the children to match the words with the notes they hear.
- Vary the dynamics by asking the children to sing loudly, quietly, crescendo (getting louder) or decrescendo (getting softer). They could vary the tempo by singing faster or slower. Vary the timbre by using different qualities of sounds or vary the texture by using several sounds at the same time.

Starting points

- Rhythm boxes are a useful way of introducing musical notation. Here is *Chips with gravy* in rhythm notation:

Here is *Yummy, yummy, in my tummy*.

- Make a copy of the boxes below.

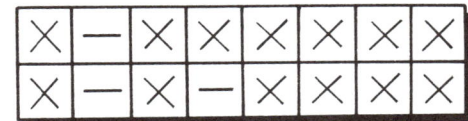
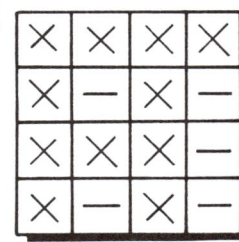

- Read each line at a time. Each cross represents a beat to play or to clap. A silent beat is represented by a – . You can say 'shh' or open out your hands to represent the silent beat. (This is particularly useful if you are clapping a rhythm, as a clap only lasts for one 'beat'.)
- Copy the rhythm boxes on to card and play the complete rhymes while maintaining a steady beat.
- Turn the cards round different ways, for instance, upside down, for further practise in music reading. The rhythms could be used to accompany songs that go with a regular 'one–two' beat, such as *Polly put the kettle on*.

Taking it further

- Take one word or phrase from the chant and use it as an 'ostinato' accompaniment. Explain to the children that it is obstinate, it won't go away! The whole chant can then be sung or played over the top of this several times.
- Use the chant as a round. Divide the children into two groups. The second group starts singing when the first group gets to the words *Rice pudding*.
- The whole chant could form the first section in a much longer structure. Here is a middle section to make the piece longer.

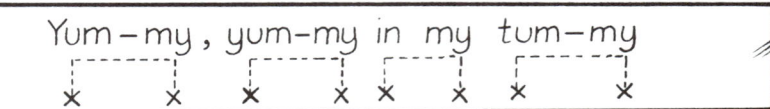

Put it all together to make a very long piece of music that goes like this:

What's for dinner?

- Match the correct notes with the words.

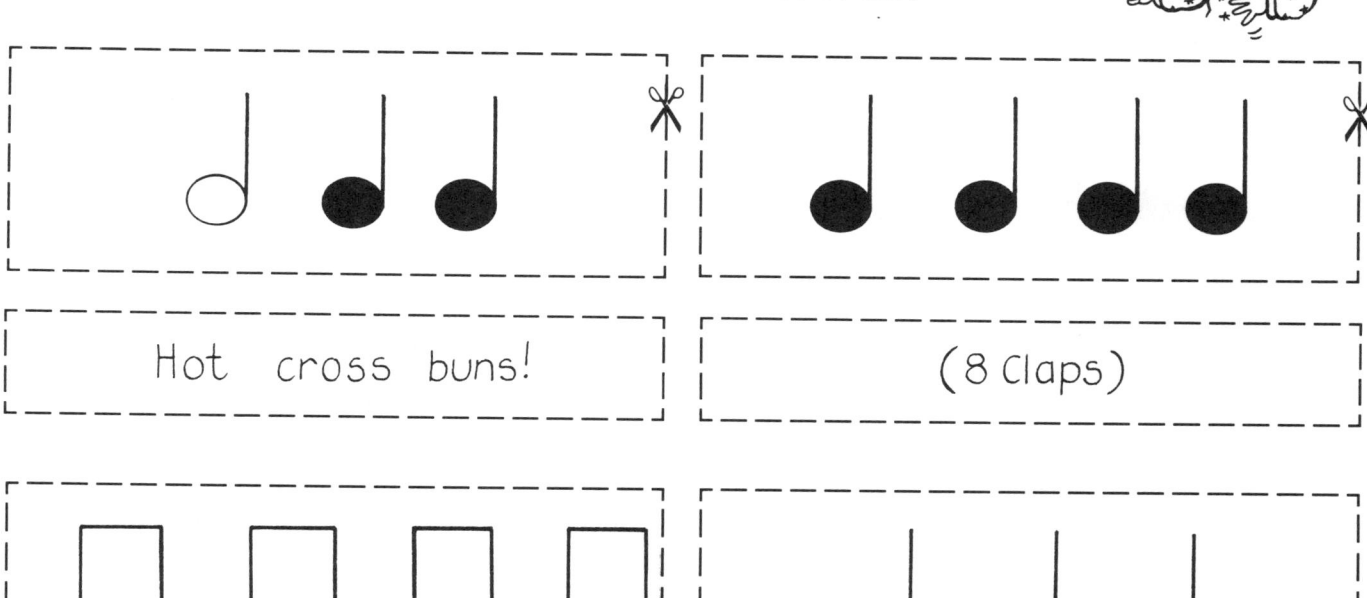

| Hot   cross   buns! | (8 Claps) |

| Chips   with   gra-vy | Baked   beans |

| Yum-my, yum-my in my tum-my | (8 Claps) |

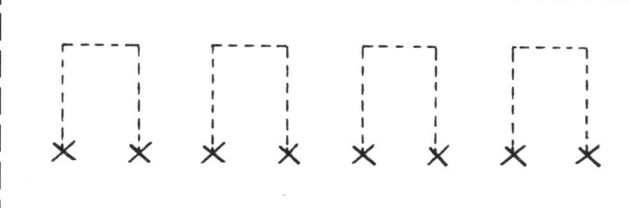

| Rice   pud-ding | Yum-my, yum-my in my tum-my |

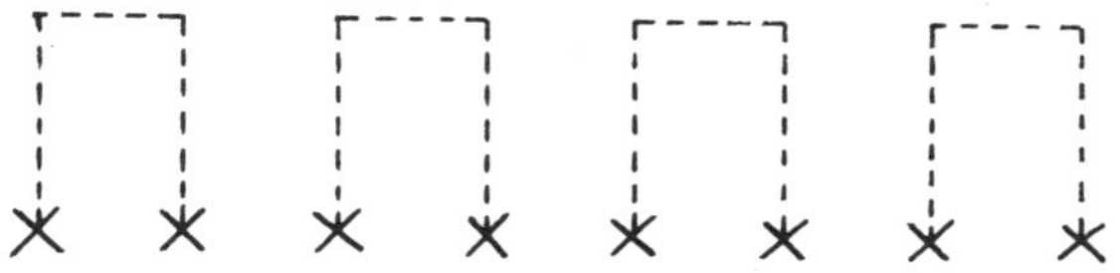

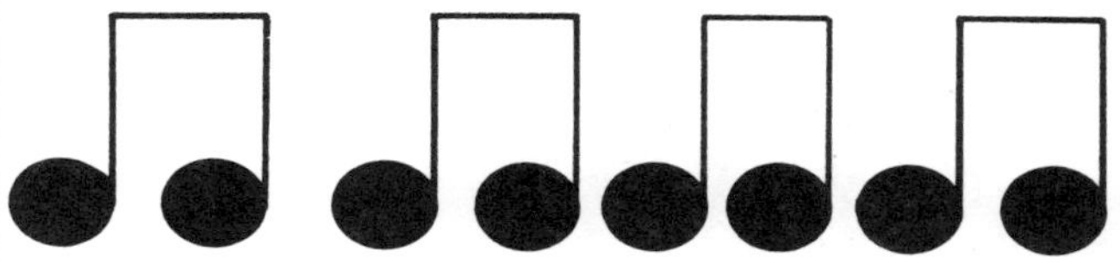

Rap in the kitchen – Ideas page

Key idea
- To develop rhythmic awareness.

Activities
- Music inspired by the West Indies is renowned for its rhythmic variety and vitality. Sing the traditional song *Mango Walk*. Listen to *Jamaican Rumba* by Arthur Benjamin. Encourage the children to join in with the music using classroom instruments.
- Ask them to make shakers out of old cartons. When these are filled with small pebbles they will sound like maracas. (Remember to secure the tops carefully!)
- Does each shaker have an individual sound? The children could experiment with different-sized containers and different contents, including sand, dried peas, rice and so on.
- They could decorate each shaker with a carnival sticker made from the patterns on the activity page. Remind them to put their name on the sticker and then use the shaker in their rap.
- Divide the children into small groups and encourage them to write their own rap song.

Starting points
- It's great fun to make a rap. Read these three raps to the children.

Indian pepper salad rap

Fresh red pepper and red tomato,
Four fresh chillies and a cucumber.
Add half an onion, pepper spice,
Then mix with vinegar to make it nice!

Breakfast rap

"Morning dad, my tum is empty,
What's for breakfast now I'm up?"
"Juice and toast
And jam and honey,
But you must do the washing up!"

Just a snack rap

Just a snack is all I want,
I'll open the fridge to see what's there.
There's bread and cheese
And a squashy, ripe banana
And food for the cat, for Dave
And for Claire.

- Ask them to tap out a very steady pulse and then say the words from one of the raps in time to the beat. Encourage them to keep going until they get a catchy rhythm in their voice.
- Keep a steady beat in the background. Use the rhythm section on an electric keyboard or a drum machine as a backing. This will give a precise beat. Make sure it is loud enough to be heard in the classroom. Encourage the children to add other instruments to the rap, one at a time. They could play the rhythm of the words, play rhythm patterns (*ostinato*) or do what they like (improvise!).
- The children will need to decide how to start and stop the rap and when to add instruments and voices. Do they need a conductor?

Carnival stickers

- Colour in the carnival stickers.
- Write your name on each sticker.

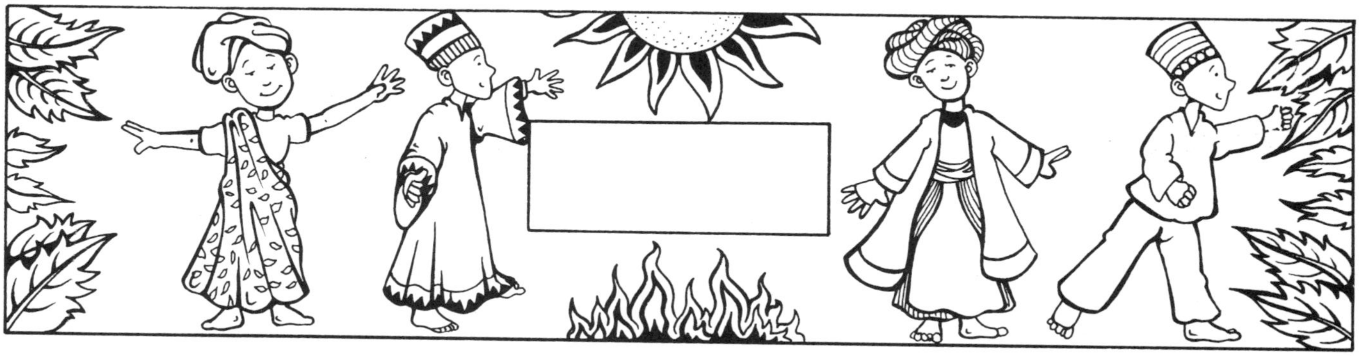

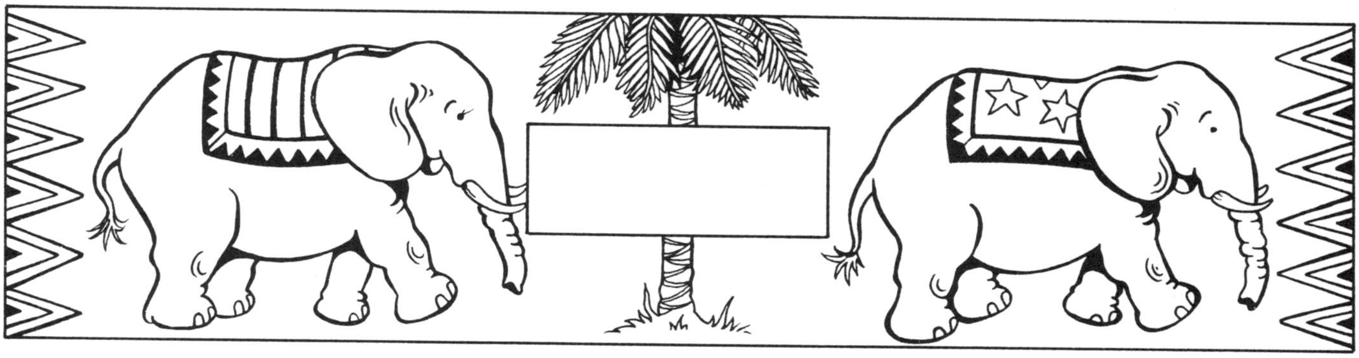

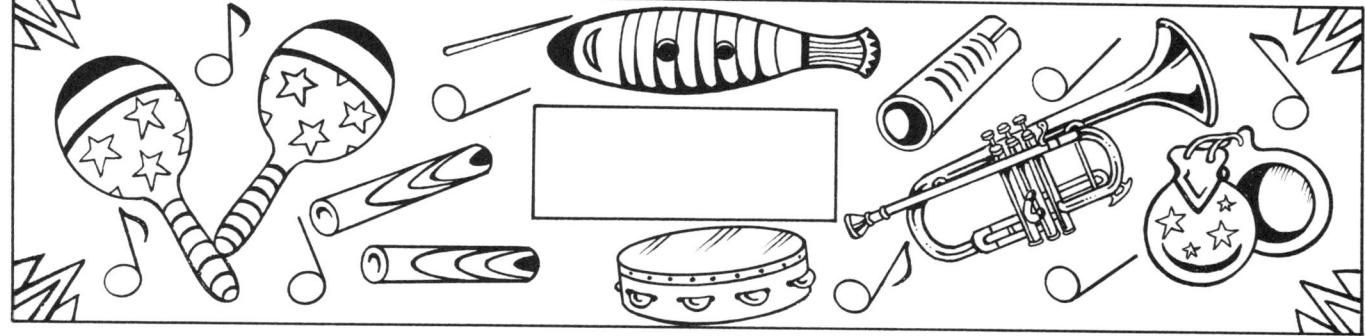

 • Decorate your shaker with the stickers.

Keeping time! – Ideas page

Key idea

- To count in twos and threes to develop a sense of pulse and rhythm.

Activities

- The Counting Clown can count in twos and threes. Ask the children to cut out the juggling balls on the activity page. The television screen should be used for more able children.
- Play a piece of music and ask them to choose the correct number of balls (and the correct television screen) to match the number of beats they heard.
- When the Counting Clown hears music that goes in twos, he juggles with two balls and looks at a television screen that shows 2/4 (2 crotchet beats to a bar).

- When he hears music that goes in threes, he juggles with three balls and looks at a television screen that shows 3/4 (3 crotchet beats to a bar).

- Repeat this exercise with different pieces of music.

Starting points

- Explain to the children that most music has a steady beat and that you can count in twos, three or fours to it. Sing *Polly put the kettle on* and ask them whether the beats go in twos or threes. (The beats go in twos, but it could be two sets of two, making fours.)
- Now sing it to numbers. (This is quite difficult!)

Pol -ly   put   the   ket -tle   on,
One and two   and one and two
Pol -ly   put   the   ket -tle   on,
One and two   and one and two
Pol -ly   put   the   ket -tle   on, we'll
One and two   and one and two and
All   have   tea.
One   two   one   (two)

- The children could march to the music, 'left–right, left–right' and move their hands.
- Now sing:

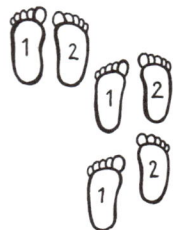

Lav - en - der's blue, did-dle, did-dle,
One two three one two and three and
Lav - en - der's green.
One two three one (two three)
When I am King, did-dle, did-dle,
One two three one two and three and
You shall be Queen.
One two three one (two three)

Ask the children whether the beats go in twos or threes. (They go in threes.) Sing it to numbers as above. (This is even harder!) The children could move their hands to the music 'down–right–up'.

Taking it further

- Play some tunes and ask the children whether the beats go in twos or threes. For example, *Oranges and lemons* (threes), *Mary, Mary, quite contrary* (twos), *London's burning* (threes), *Sing a song of sixpence* (twos), and *Close every door to me* (threes) and *I closed my eyes* (twos) from *Joseph and the Amazing Technicolour Dreamcoat*.
- It is important that the children respond by listening to the music. Looking at a musical score can sometimes be confusing for a non-musician.
- Do the same with some recorded instrumental music. A useful guide is that most marches go in twos and waltzes go in threes (but again listen carefully).

IDEAS BANK – *Songs and Rhymes*   © Folens

The Counting Clown

The Counting Clown can count in twos and threes.
- Listen to the music. Do the beats go in twos or threes?

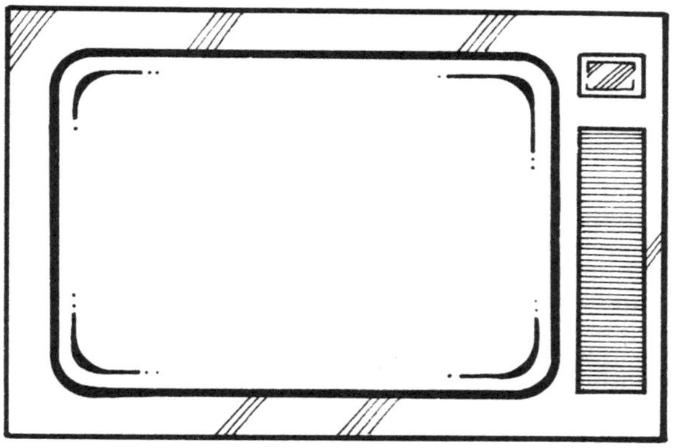

- Cut out and use these pictures to match the beats.

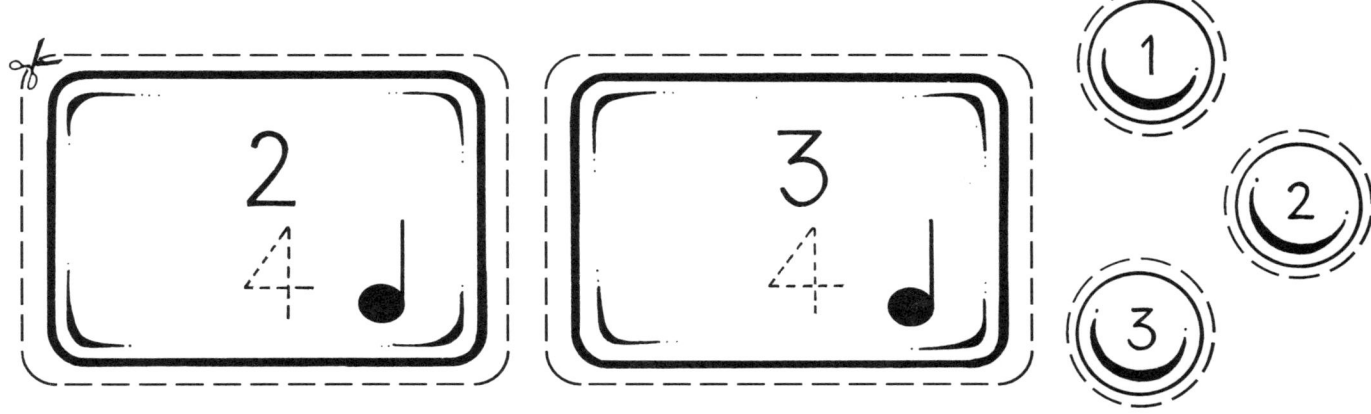

Rhymes in music – Ideas page

Key idea

- To develop musical patterns out of short rhymes and sayings.

Starting points

- Use the sayings 'Look before you leap' and 'Too many cooks spoil the broth' to make a musical chant. Rhymes and sayings are an interesting and rich resource for musical performance and composition.
- Ask the children to say 'Look before you leap' until it comes out in a rhythm. Then ask them to clap and say the rhyme at the same time.
- Then encourage them to match (echo) the spoken word by clapping. The sounds are now ready to be transferred to instruments, untuned or tuned.
- Do the same with the saying 'Too many cooks spoil the broth'. It will prompt a different rhythm. This can be emphasised with a contrasting instrumental colour (timbre).
- Play one of the rhythms. Ask the children to say which one it is. Change the instrumentation, but keep to the identical rhythm pattern. Can the children still tell which rhythm is which?

Activities

- The ability to complete a rhyme is essential to a child's development. Supplying the correct word can be backed up by the addition of a musical rhythm, such as the beat of a drum.
- Ask the children to complete the rhymes on the activity page.

'I sail on a pond, I always float,
I've a mast and a deck, and I'm a boat'

'Fun to handle, fun to hold,
But if I break, consider me sold'

'East, west, home's best'

'Whatever the day, whatever the time,
It's never too late to think up a rhyme'

- Say the first completed rhyme on the activity page while clapping the beats at the same time.
- Encourage the children to say each rhyme and to complete the beats in the space beneath.
- They could write the missing word in a different colour.
- Ask the children to play the whole phrase on an instrument as you say the rhyme, or the other way round.
- Alternatively play the first part of each rhyme on one instrument and play the missing word on a contrasting instrument.
- Make rhyme cards from the activity page to be used by the children working in pairs.

Taking it further

- Make up a complete piece of music based on the rhythms suggested by two of these sayings.

One structure is to use the first rhyme followed by its echo, then the second rhyme followed by its echo and finally ending with the first rhyme's echo. There are many other combinations the children could experiment with.
- Other suggestions include using one rhyme as an ostinato pattern all the way through the piece. Introduce dynamics, such as loud, soft, crescendo (getting louder), decrescendo or diminuendo (getting softer).
- The children could make a musical score of their piece.

IDEAS BANK – *Songs and Rhymes* © Folens

Rhymes to complete

- Fill in the missing beats.
- Fill in the missing word to complete the rhymes.

Nice red apple, round and sweet,
Nice to look at, good to eat

I sail on a pond, I always float,
I've a mast and a deck, and I'm a boat

Fun to handle, fun to hold,
But if I break, consider me . . .

East, west, home's . . .

Whatever the day, whatever the time,
It's never too late to think up a . . .

Pitch ideas – two notes – Ideas page

Key idea
- To learn to discriminate between two notes.

Starting points
- Use two notes, for instance, C and A or G and E and play a simple pattern. Ask the children whether the notes they hear are 'high–high–high–low' or 'high–high–low–low'.
- Play the notes and sing either 'high' or 'low' or say the letter names of the notes as you play them. If you use individual chime bars, hold them up and use the beater in a distinctive manner.
- Choose some of the children to play with you on individual chime bars. The rest can play imaginary 'magic' bars. Make sure that all the children get a turn to play!

Activities
- Place some chime bars over the correct places on the ladder on the activity page. Then play the notes as one of the children points to them.
- You can then point to the written notes **first** and then sing or play them. This is more complicated, but will help the children to develop the ability to 'think' notes.
- Try echo playing (follow my leader) using just two notes. You will need to start this off.
- As a stimulus, ask the children to think of words or phrases as they play, for example, 'high–high–low' or 'high–low–low' and so on. Keep the music very simple to begin with.
- Ask the children to use the words of *London Bridge is falling down* to make a two-note tune.
- They could select their own high and low notes. Will they start their tune with a high or a low note? Is the pattern the same all the way through? How can the words 'My fair lady' at the end be set?

Taking it further
- Divide the children into groups and give them one of the following 'spelling aids' to make into a two-note tune.

Difficulty
Mrs D, Mrs I, Mrs F F I, Mrs C, Mrs U, Mrs L T Y.

Receive
'Mr R, Mr E, Mr C, Mr E, Mr I, Mr V, Mr E, RECEIVE!'

Spelling aid
I before E, except after C.

- They should repeat their phrase until a rhythm emerges. Then, as they play on their two notes, they will find that they have a tune. Encourage them to sing or hum quietly as they play.
- The children will probably remember their tunes quite easily. If not, they could write down the letter names of the pitch notes using the pitch ladder on page 33. This shows the order of the notes. The highest notes are always on the top of the ladder. They could then turn the ladder round so that these high notes are on the right.

High and low

High

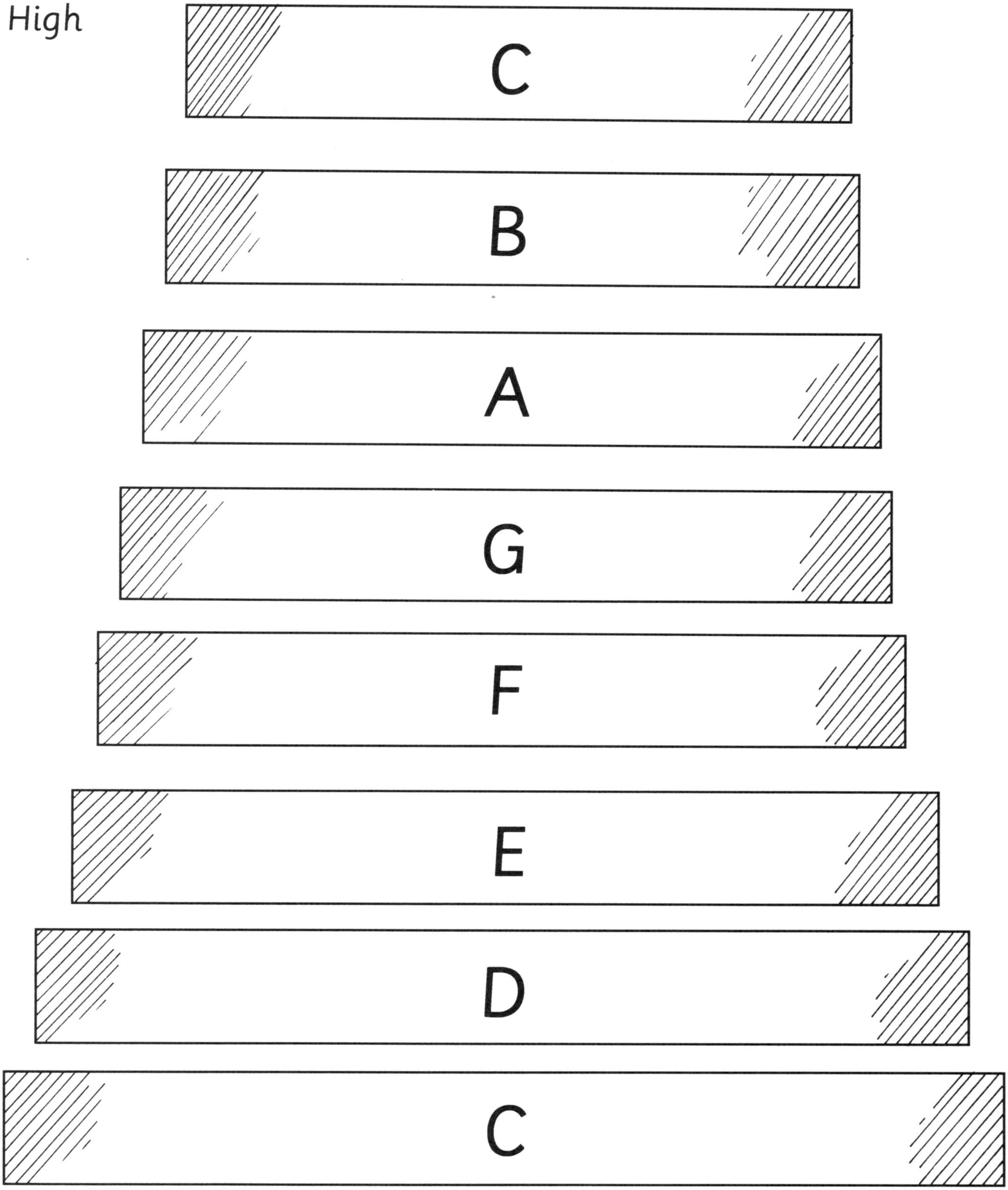

　　　　C

　　　　B

　　　　A

　　　　G

　　　　F

　　　　E

　　　　D

　　　　C

Low

© Folens (copiable page)   IDEAS BANK – *Songs and Rhymes*

Pitch ideas – three notes – Ideas page

Key idea

- To learn to discriminate between three notes.

Starting points

- Start with three contrasting and widely spaced notes on a tuned percussion instrument (or use three individual chime bars, high–middle–low). Play the three notes at random and ask the children which notes they heard.
- Use the three notes to illustrate a story with three characters, such as *The Three Bears* or *The Three Billy Goats Gruff*. Each character should be represented by a different sound. For instance, Baby Bear could be represented by the highest note, Daddy Bear by the lowest and so on.

Play the character's note either just before they speak, while they are speaking or just after. This will help the children to associate a specific pitched sound with a character.
- Play the groups of notes above and ask the children to identify which note is high, which is low and so on.

Activities

- Play three notes, such as G (high), E (middle) and C (low). Sing the words 'Listen to my song'. Then play the notes as you sing 'high–middle–low, high–middle–low'. Then sing 'What did I play?' and the children should sing the sequence back to you, 'high–middle–low, high–middle–low'.
- Now try playing the notes in a different order. (Don't make it too complicated!) Later, you could add more words.
- Ask the children to make up their own three-note song. Divide them into pairs and give them a copy of the blank musical stave and the noteheads that appear on the activity page. (Make additional notes if needed.)
- The children could place the notes on the stave and then point, play or sing. The relative pitch of the sounds is more important than the correct letter names of the note. For example they could just sing 'high–high–low–middle'.

Taking it further

- Alternatively, make a graphic score based on three pitched notes. Write this score on a board or card. Play the tune on the score or ask one of the children to point to each pitch as you play.
- The children will enjoy drawing graphic scores for their own three-note tunes. There is an example below.
- Encourage them to experiment with these high, middle and low sounds. They could try turning their score upside down and then play the tune!

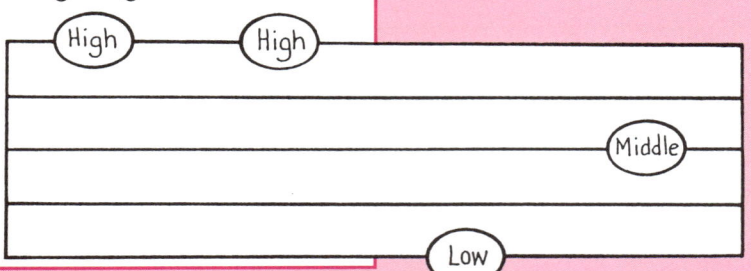

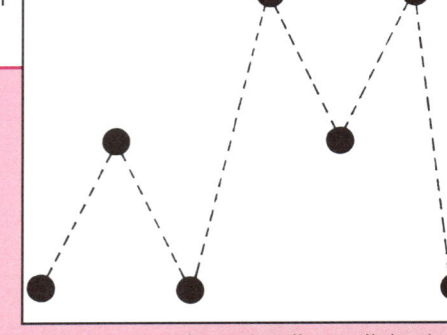

A graphic score based on three pitched notes.

High – middle – low

- Put the notes on the musical stave.

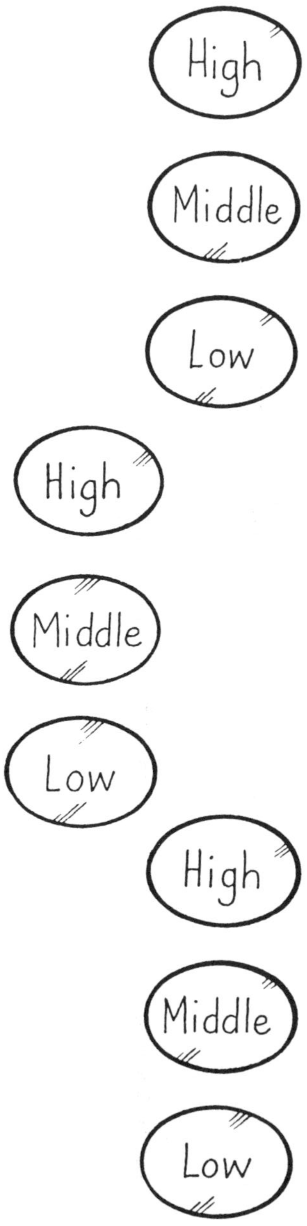

(High) (Middle) (Low)   (High) (Middle) (Low)   (High) (Middle) (Low)

High · · · · Low

 • Play or sing your tune.

IDEAS BANK – *Songs and Rhymes*

© Folens (copiable page)

High and low – *Ideas page*

Key idea

- To explore the use of high and low sounds.

Taking it further

- Ask the children how they will remember their song. They could tape record it or make a drawing of the tune using graphic notation to show the highs and lows in picture form.
- Alternatively, encourage them to write down the letter names of the notes they use. They could use the pitch ladders to help find where the notes are.
- They could then try playing their song on an instrument while reading these notes.
- For more able children, introduce the third pitch ladder on the activity page. This is called 'Tonic Solfa' and is another useful aid to learning about pitch. On the pitch ladder below, doh is C and so on.

Tonic Solfa

Note scale

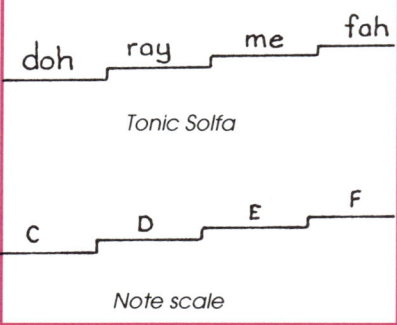

Starting points

- Ask the children to identify high and low sounds in their environment. Use instruments, voices and so on to demonstrate these sounds. Here are some examples:

High and low notes on a keyboard

High and low notes on tuned percussion

High sounds outside

Singing high

Low sounds outside

Singing low

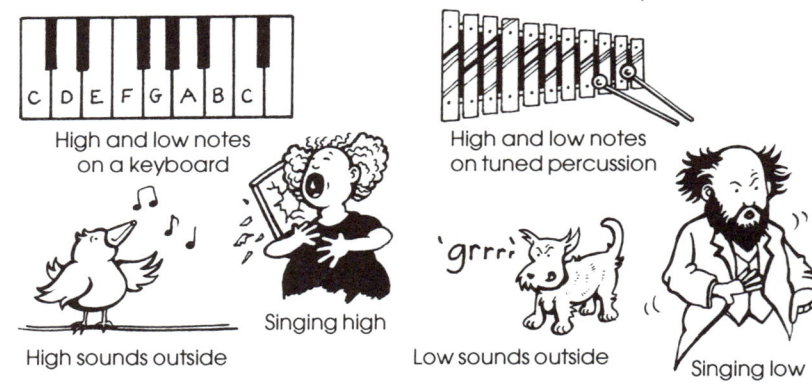

- Ask them to listen carefully to these sounds. Which are 'high'? Which are 'low'? Which is the highest sound?

Activities

- Make up a tune for *Kitten on the roof top* using low and high sounds such as C and G.
- As you sing, point out low and high parts of the song. Encourage the children to join in with you.
- Sing the rhyme *Jack and Jill* and point out the low and high parts of the song, for instance 'went up the hill' and so on.
- Give the children a copy of the activity page and ask them to point to the correct place on the first or second pitch ladder as you sing or play.
- Make up a tune for the words of *The King of France*. For the first two lines you could use all the ascending notes of the scale C D E F G A B C. For lines three and four use the notes in descending order. Ask the children to select an instrument and use one of the pitch ladders to help them compose their tune.

Kitten on the roof top

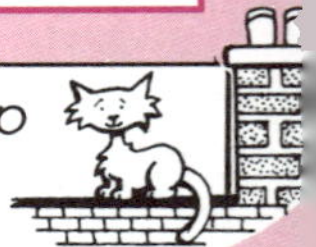

C G
Kitten on the roof top,

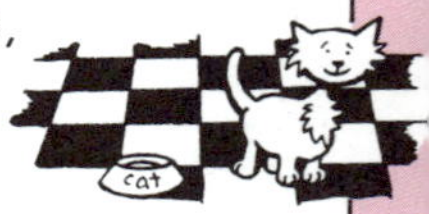

G C
kitten on the floor.

C G
Kitten jumping up and up, then

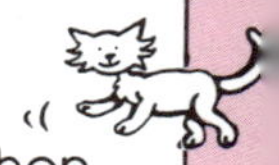

C C
down she goes once more.

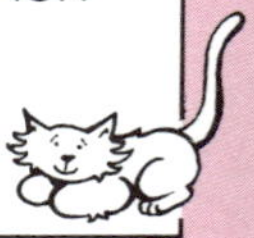

The King of France

The King of France went up the hill
With twenty thousand men.
The King of France came down the hill
And ne'er went up again.

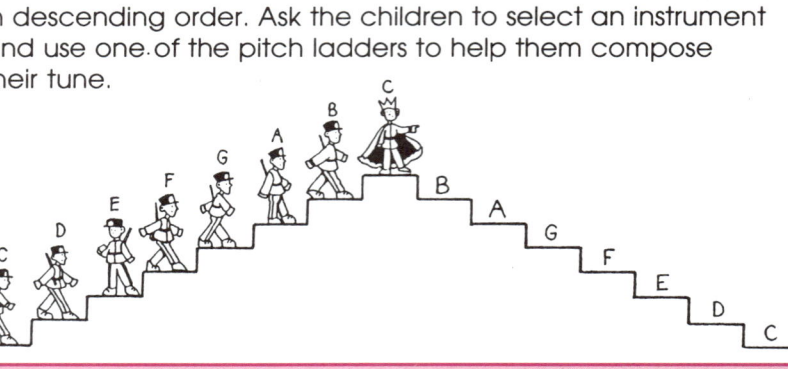

Pitch ladders

- Use one of these pitch ladders to help you make a tune.

More sets of notes – Ideas page

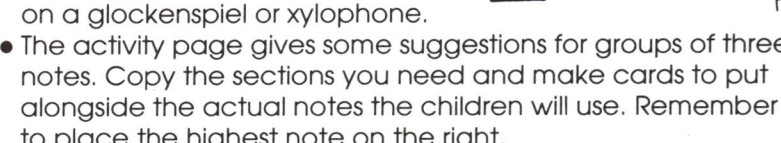

Key idea

- To use more notes to make up tunes for songs and rhymes.

Starting points

- Play three notes on individual chime bars or on individual bars on a glockenspiel or xylophone.
- The activity page gives some suggestions for groups of three notes. Copy the sections you need and make cards to put alongside the actual notes the children will use. Remember to place the highest note on the right.
- Select some words to use and say them over to yourself. Then play the notes and put the words and sounds together. Experiment and repeat parts as desired.
- You could add a simple accompaniment on percussion instruments.

Activities

- Ask the children to set the days of the week to music. They should start with just two notes, such as G and E.

  ```
  G           E
  Mon    —   day
  Tues   —   day
  Wednes —   day
  Thurs  —   day
  ```

- They could then make up a song using three notes, such as G, E and C. Use the poem *My week!* (opposite) as an example.
- Then ask them to make a song out of the words of the rhyme *Sneeze on Monday*. They could use the notes E, G and A.

My week!

	G	E	G		C
Mon —	day		What a		day
Tues —	day		Out to		play
Wednes —	day		Hurt my		leg
Thurs —	day		Stayed in		bed
Fri —	day		Back at		school
Satur —	day		Oh so		cool
Sun —	day		Special		day
Seven	days		make my		week

Solomon Grundy

Solomon Grundy, born on Monday,
Christened on Tuesday,
Married on Wednesday.
Took ill on Thursday, worse on Friday,
Died on Saturday, buried on Sunday,
So that was the end of Solomon Grundy.

- *Solomon Grundy* gives plenty of scope for musical interpretation. Something different happens on each day of the week, so encourage the children to let their music bring this out. They could make a musical setting that has its own, free rhythm, independent of the words and then play this instrumental piece by itself!

Sneeze on Monday

G   A G E G   A G E
Sneeze on Monday, sneeze for danger,
Sneeze on Tuesday, miss a stranger,
Sneeze on Wednesday, get a letter,
Sneeze on Thursday, something better,
Sneeze on Friday, sneeze for sorrow,
Sneeze on Saturday, see you tomorrow.

Taking it further

- Ask the children to make tongue-twisters into songs (see below). They could use two or three notes.
- Encourage them to sing the words slowly at first. (It is often easier to sing things than to say them.)

How many cookies could a good cook cook,
If a good cook could cook cookies?
As many cookies as a good cook could cook,
If a good cook could cook cookies.

She sells sea shells on the sea shore.

IDEAS BANK – Songs and Rhymes   © Folens

Sets of notes

- Make up a tune for a song or rhyme.
- Which notes will you use?

C	E	G		F	A	C
G	B	D		C	D	E
D	E	G		E	G	A
F	G	B		C	F#	G

Sailing and playing – Ideas page

Key idea

- To invent and refine musical performances based on traditional games.

Starting points

- Sing the following song.

    My ship sailed from China with a cargo of tea,
    All laden with presents for you and for me.
    They brought me a fan, just imagine my bliss
    When I found myself going like this, like this ...

- Now keep the words the same, but change the actions each time. For instance, sing it again and during the final line wave one hand across the body. Sing it again and wave two hands to cross over the body. Then cross one foot over the other ankle and finally cross both feet over each other.
- Then sing the song in two groups, alternating each 'verse'. Ask one group to continue to sing 'like this' with the actions, while the other group goes on to the next 'verse'.
- Use a hand clap or a rhythm instrument to keep a steady beat.

Activities

- *The big bass drum* is a traditional cumulative ring game played with different instruments. For each verse a new instrument is added to the list of the previous ones.
- Cut out and enlarge the instrument cards on the activity page. Hold them up to show which instrument is added next as the children sing the song. (Fold the words over if you don't want the children to read the words.)

    Oh, we can play on the big bass drum
    And this is the music to it;
    Boom, boom, boom goes the big bass drum,
    And that's the way we do it.

- One possible order to sing the song could be the big bass drum card followed by the violin, glockenspiel, bass guitar, saxophone and then tambourine card.
- You could add different instruments to the game by holding up a classroom instrument or making a card for it.

Taking it further

- Sing this song. It is a 'thread the needle' game.

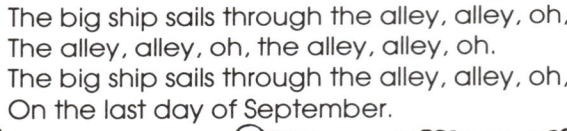

The big ship sails through the alley, alley, oh,
The alley, alley, oh, the alley, alley, oh.
The big ship sails through the alley, alley, oh,
On the last day of September.

- The children join hands for the first verse. The child at one end of the line puts a hand on the wall. As everyone sings, the child at the other end of the line leads the line through the arch or 'alley' at the wall end, forcing the child with their hand on the wall to turn round. The game continues, as the first verse is repeated, until all the children are turned round in this way.
- Sing the second verse in a circle, 'We all dip our heads in the deep blue sea' and so on. Ask the children to dip their heads down. Their fingers should be wagging for verse three, 'The captain said, "This will never, never do" ...'. The fourth verse 'The big ship sank to the bottom of the sea ...' can be sung with appropriate actions.
- A group of children could form a rhythm group to play during the game to give the song a nice catchy swing!

IDEAS BANK – Songs and Rhymes © Folens

Oh, we can play on the big bass drum ...

Big bass drum	Violin	Glockenspiel
Boom, boom, boom	Fiddle, dee, dee	Ping, ping, ping
Bass guitar	Saxophone	Tambourine
Dum, dum, dum	Doobee, doobee, doo	Tam, tam, tam

Forest music – Ideas page

Key idea

- To explore stimuli for performing and composing ideas.

Activities

- Divide the children into groups and give each one a copy of the graphic score on the activity page. The score is based on the ideas in the rhyme *Going on a journey*, such as waking up, travelling and finally arriving.
- The children should decide which sound sources they will need. They could use their own voices, body sounds, untuned and tuned percussion instruments and so on, to create different effects.
- They should practise each section of the graphic score separately. How long will each section last?
- They must decide how the sounds of each section will fit together. Encourage them to follow the score as they join each section and the journey progresses. They could go back over some parts of the journey and repeat them if they want.
- Encourage them to sing a song during part of their journey since they will be feeling happy!
- Ask the children why their 'journey music' will sound different each time it is played.

Starting points

- Ask the children to think about how they feel first thing on the morning of a journey. Are they excited? Does the journey take a long time? Are they tired when they arrive? What do they do as soon as they arrive?
- Read the rhyme below and fill the words in brackets with different examples.

Going on a journey

We get up early to pack our bags …
It's holiday time – what a lot of fun.
Off in (*a plane*) to (*the destination*) …
When we're there we'll see the sun!

- Sounds can echo the rhythm or the mood of each line. For instance the going up or down in a plane and so on.
- The children could create some sound effect recordings of travel sounds or find some songs about journeys.

Taking it further

- Encourage the children to make their own music based on the *Forest song*. It can be sung to a two-note pattern (G, E) or a three-note pattern (A, G, E). Alternatively the tune of *Five little fishes* fits the words nicely. Replace the words in brackets with other examples.

Forest song
Deep in the forest in the middle of the night
I saw a (*lion*) who gave me a fright!
The (*lion*) went (*replace with five repeated sounds*)
And I went singing on my way.
Du du dubee dubee dubee du
Du du dubee dubee dubee du
Du du dubee dubee dubee du
And I went singing on my way.

Deep in the forest in the middle of the day
I saw a (*rabbit*) who wanted to play.
The (*rabbit*) went (*replace with five repeated sounds*)
And I went singing on my way.
Du du dubee dubee dubee du *and so on.*

- They could make up new verses and alternate the 'night' and 'day' sections to create a longer song. Remind them to put a 'Du du dubee' chorus between each verse.
- Add instrumental sound effects while some children sing or clap. A rhythm group could provide a catchy backing.

IDEAS BANK – *Songs and Rhymes*

Journey music

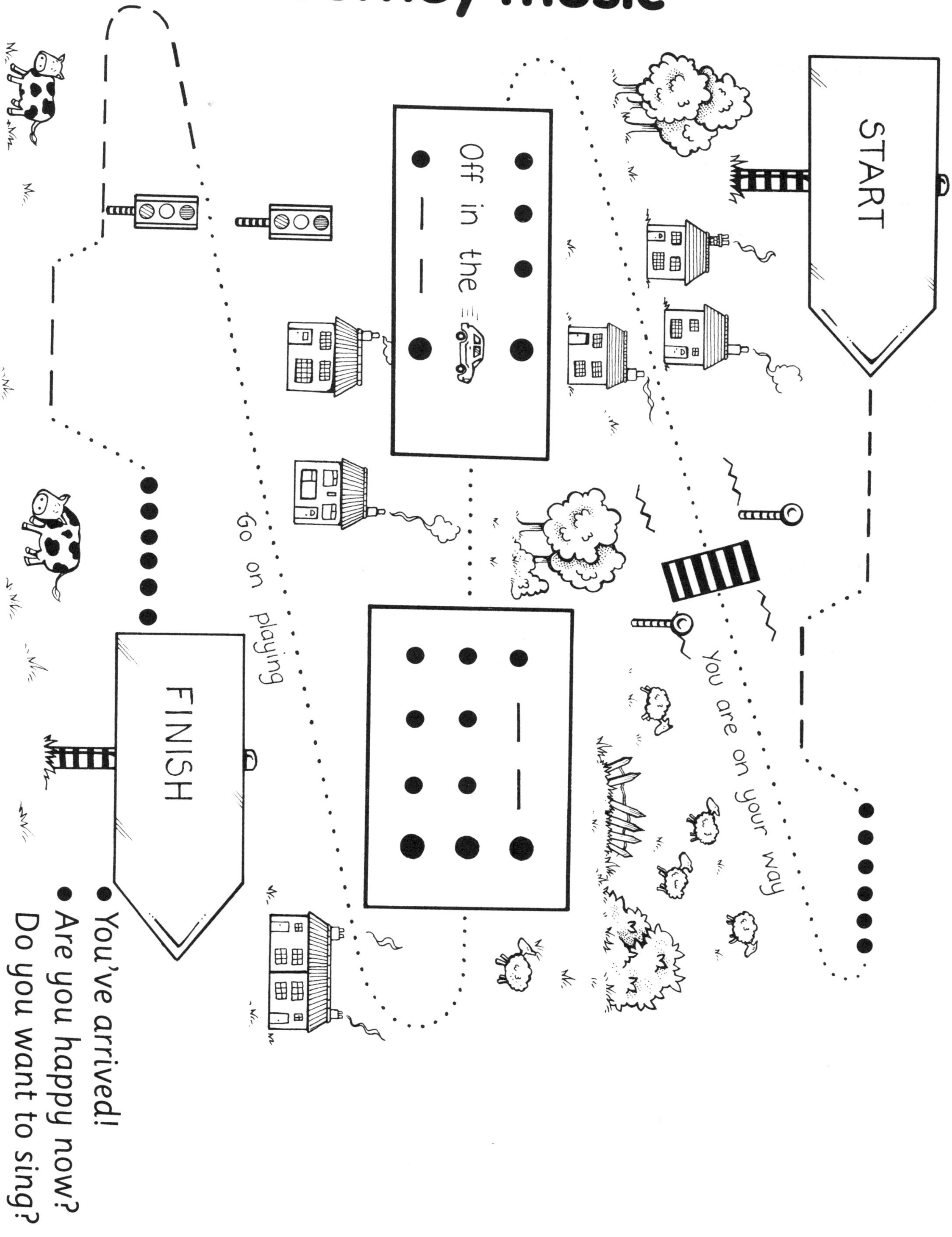

Off in the

START

You are on your way

Go on playing

FINISH
- You've arrived!
- Are you happy now?
- Do you want to sing?

© Folens (copiable page)   IDEAS BANK – *Songs and Rhymes*

Lullaby baby – Ideas page

Key idea
- To use stimulus of a lullaby for performing and composing ideas.

Sul — la D E
Lul — la D E
Sul — la D E
Lul — la D E

Starting points
- Ask the children to think about how they would encourage a small baby to go to sleep. For instance, would they rock the baby's cradle slowly, fast or fairly slowly? Would they sing loudly or softly to the baby?
- Ask them to imagine they are rocking the cradle up and down with a regular motion. As they rock, they should say 'Sulla, lulla' over and over again, keeping the pulse very steady.
- Give them a copy of the activity page and encourage them to use the ideas on it to create a soothing lullaby. Begin by playing just two notes (such as D and E) as the children sing 'Sulla, lulla'. Encourage some children to join in by playing the two notes very quietly to make a rocking pattern.
- Add some more words, such as:

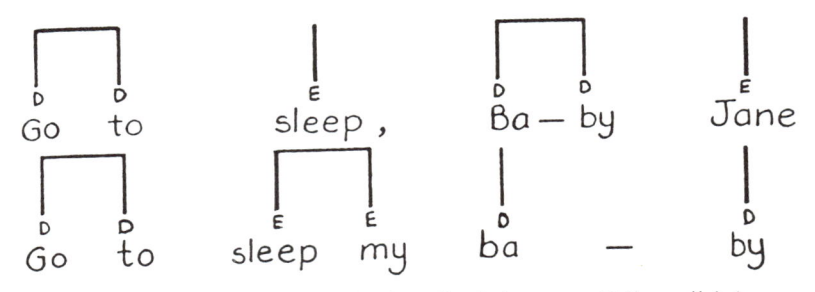

  Go (D) to (D) sleep (E), Ba (D) — by (D) Jane (E)
  Go (D) to (D) sleep (E) my (E) ba (D) — by (D)

- Encourage them to keep singing their tune until they think the baby would be asleep. Then they should stop singing the words, but continue to hum the tune a few more times.
- Record their music and play it back to them. Is it soothing? Encourage them to write down their tune.

Activities
- The *Nurse's song* from the *Oxford Treasury of Children's Poems* (1991) used to be sung when many people lived in the country. Divide the children into groups and ask them to make up a tune to match the words.
- Again encourage them to use some of the patterns on the activity page to give them ideas. (The notes G and E are useful to begin with.)
- Remind them that the music must sound very soothing. They could choose some classroom instruments to accompany the song and could also make special sound effects for the sheep and the dog.
- Let the groups take it in turns to sing their tune while some children act out the song.

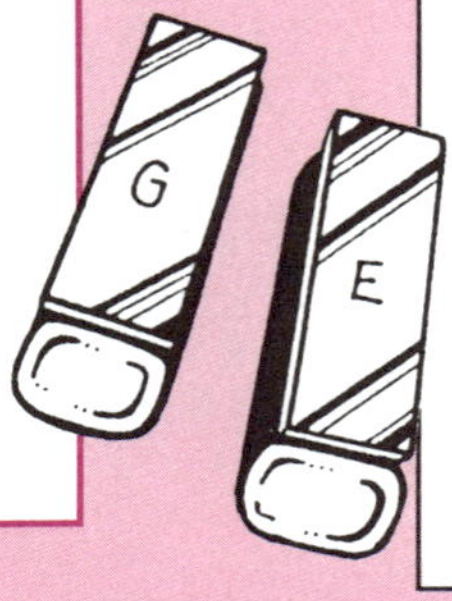

Nurse's song

Sleep, baby, sleep!
Your father herds his sheep,
Your mother shakes the little tree
From which fall pretty dreams on thee,
Sleep, baby, sleep!

Sleep, baby, sleep!
And bleat not like a sheep,
Or else the shepherd's angry dog
Will come and bite my naughty rogue,
Sleep, baby, sleep!

Sleep, baby, sleep!
Go out, you barking black dog, go,
And waken not my baby so,
Sleep, baby, sleep!

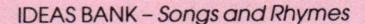

Lullaby song

- Choose two chime bars to play your lullaby.

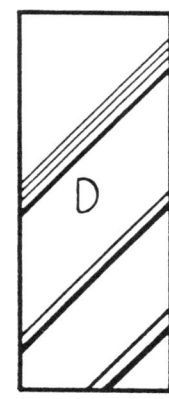

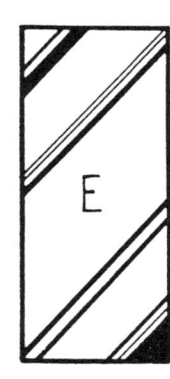

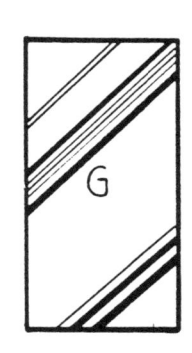

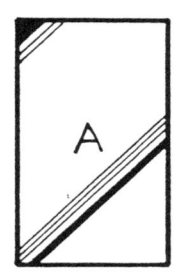

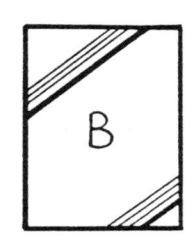

D   E   G   A   B

- Sing the words below and make a rocking pattern.

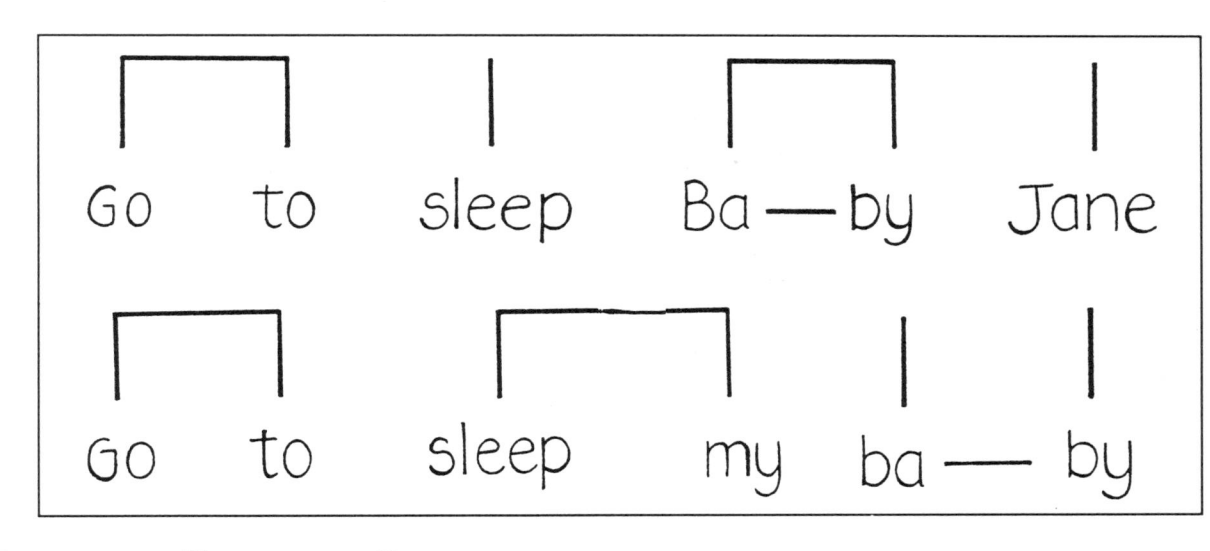

Sul — la   Lul — la   Sul — la   Lul — la

D   E   D   E   D   E   D   E

Go   to   sleep   Ba—by   Jane

Go   to   sleep   my   ba—by

D   E   D   E   D   E   D   E

Rock—ing   gent—ly   ba—by   sleep—ing

- Now make up your own lullaby.

Marching along – Ideas page

Key idea
- To learn how to respond to a steady beat.

Activities
- Enlarge the marching patterns on the activity page. Several types of musical symbols are shown including picture notation, simplified rhythm notation and traditional rhythm notation. Block out any not needed. Construct your own chart and point to the patterns as you say and play them.
- It is vital for the children to keep a very steady, regular beat and to fit the words in at the right time. Keep returning to the 'left–right' pattern at the top of the page if they get lost. They could try out some marching steps to the beat.
- Encourage the children to write down some of their own marching patterns in words and musical symbols.

Starting points
- Discuss the regular sounds the children can hear in their environment. For instance, windscreen wipers on a car, the regular 'swoosh–swoosh–gurgle' noise made by a washing machine and so on. Some clocks and watches make a regular, tick-tock sound.
- Most music has a regular beat. We can move or count to it. The following song is good to march and clap to.

Oh the Grand Old Duke of York,
He had ten thousand men.
He marched them up to the top of the hill
And he marched them down again.

And when they were up they were up,
And when they were down they were down,
And when they were only half way up
They were neither up nor down.

- The children could practise marching on the spot or round the room. Play the beat of the march using two notes on chime bars or a drum. Adjust the speed of the beat to the way they march so they get into a regular pattern.
- Encourage them to make their hands and feet march 'left–right, left–right'. Then divide them into pairs or let them march as a group. They could march in two lines, forward and back.

Marching chant

L	R	L	R	L	R
We	are	**march**ing	**down**	the	**stre**et,

L	R	L	R	L	R
Left,	right,	**left**,	right,	**go**	our **fe**et.

L	R	L	R	L	R
Left,	right,	**left**,	right,	**keep**ing	**stea**dy,

L	R	L	R	L	R
Tramping	**to**	the	**march**ing	**be**at!	

Taking it further
- Play some marches, such as *Oh when the Saints go marching in*, *Colonel Bogey* and *Pack up your troubles*. Can the children recognise the beats of the different marches?
- Select some children to play the beat of a march (the rhythm of the words or the rhythm (ostinato) patterns). They could play tuned accompaniment patterns, such as G–D for 'left–right'.
- They could make some music for the *Marching chant* (left). They will need a steady beat (not too fast) on a rhythm instrument, such as a drum or tambourine.
- Encourage them to make a musical structure for *The Grand Old Duke of York*. For instance, the march could begin with the band playing in the distance. The steady beat gets stronger as the band gets nearer. The march is played twice while some children do the actions and then it ends as the band retreats into the distance and the march gets quieter (dynamics).

IDEAS BANK – *Songs and Rhymes* © Folens

Marching patterns

- Use some of these patterns to make a march.

Left, right,   Left, right,   Left, right,   left, right

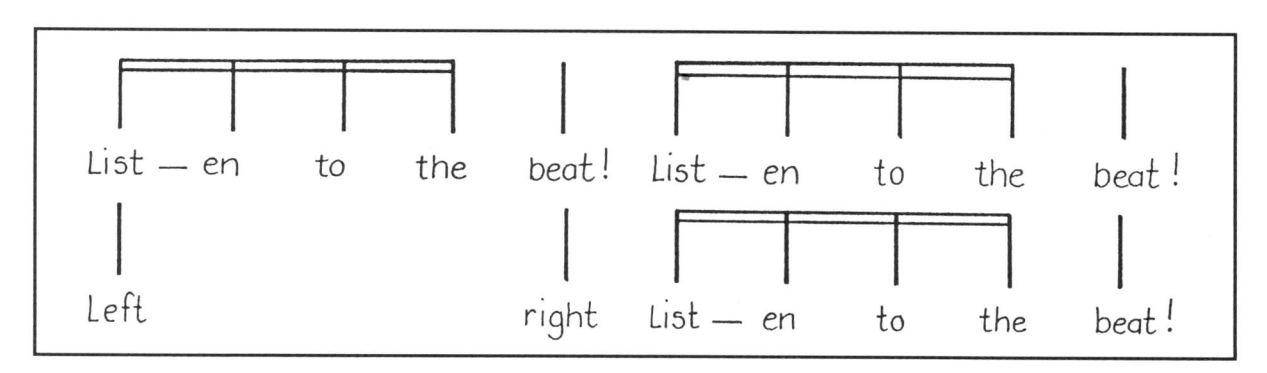

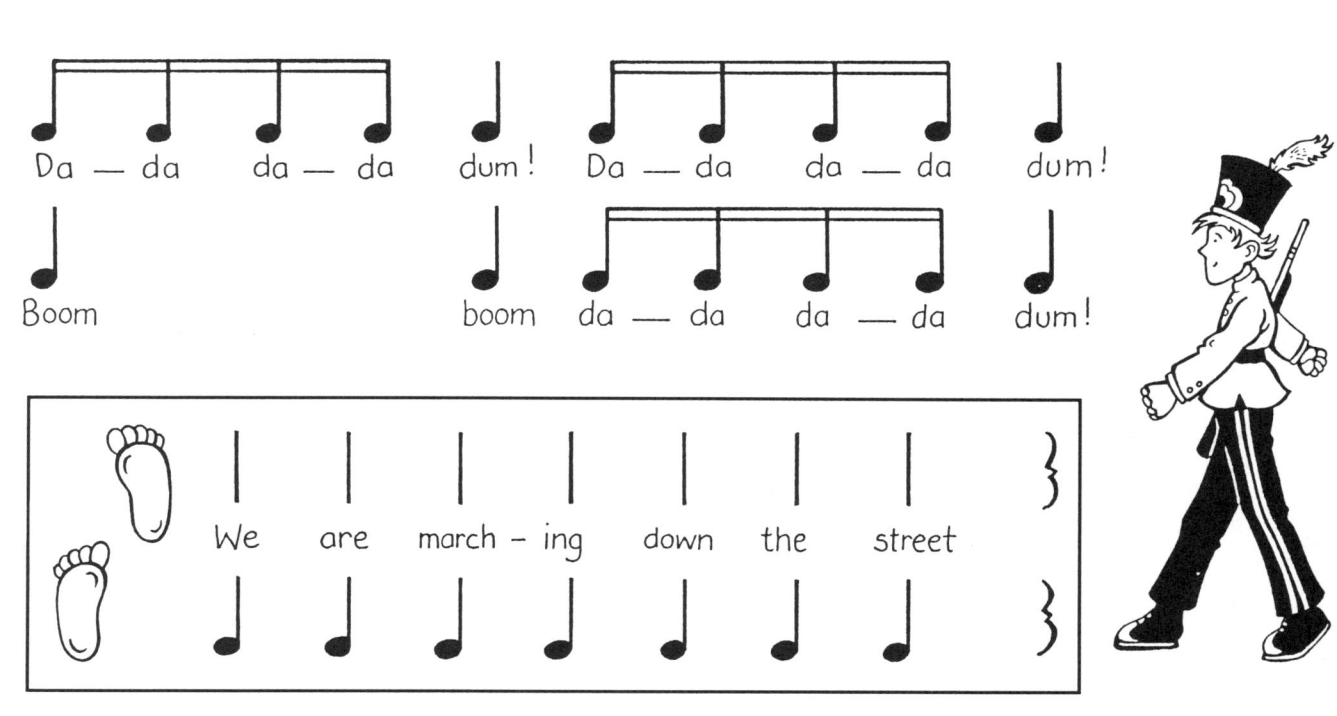

List — en to the beat! List — en to the beat!
Left   right List — en to the beat!

Da — da da — da dum! Da — da da — da dum!
Boom   boom da — da da — da dum!

We are march - ing down the street

when they were up they were up, and when they were down they were down

Contrasts – Ideas page

Key idea

- To create music depicting contrasting moods.

Starting points

- Some music can make us feel happy and some can make us feel sad. For instance, wedding music or 'quick' music could make us feel happy and memorial (funeral) music or 'slow' music could make us feel sad. Can the children think of any music that makes them both happy and sad at the same time? You can be sad to hear music that used to make you happy a long time ago!
- Sing the lines 'If you're happy and you know it clap your hands!'. Ask the children how they could make this song sound happy. What instruments could they add to make a backing rhythm all the way through to go with each action?
- Read the story of *Mr Happy* by Roger Hargreaves (Thurman Publishing Ltd) and think of suitable sound effects.

Activities

- Encourage the children to make their own music that is happy or sad. They could use the sequence of faces on the activity page that change from happy to sad. They need to match sounds to suit the mood on each face.

C A   C D

hap – py   sor – ry

- They could use different instruments to represent the change in mood or play a single instrument differently, for instance quietly for sad and so on.
- Some pitch notes and rhymes are suggested on the activity page. Remind the children that it might take a while for sad sounds to become happy ones. They need to make this mood change very slowly. Encourage them to think of some words to match their music.
- Ask some children to play their music and see if the rest of the class can guess which picture the music was composed for.

Poor Jenny is a-weeping

Poor Jenny is a-weeping,
a-weeping, a-weeping,
Poor Jenny is a-weeping,
on a bright summer's day.

I'm (she's) weeping for a
sweetheart *and so on.*

Now Jenny choose your
bridesmaids *and so on.*

Now Jenny choose
a page-boy *and so on.*

Oh, why are you weeping
a-weeping, a-weeping,
Oh, why are you weeping
on a bright summer's day?

Stand up and choose your
sweetheart *and so on.*

Now Jenny choose the
parson *and so on.*

Now Jenny shall be
married *and so on.*

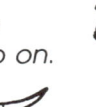

Taking it further

- *Poor Jenny is a-weeping* begins as a sad song, but the mood changes by the end. When this song is played in the traditional manner the singing reflects the change of mood from sad to happy. Ask the children to try this. Encourage them to think of different sounds to add to the song.
- They could choose different instruments to keep a steady beat. These should sound sad at first, but later should be played with a brighter sound quality (timbre) to match the change of mood.
- Add the instruments before the start of the song and then play them between each verse.
- At the end of the song, the children could 'la, la' the last verse while the instrumentalists play a very happy processional march to the wedding celebrations. Have any of the children been to a wedding? Ask them to describe the mood.

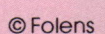

Happy and sad

- Make some music to match the faces below.

- Use these examples to help you.

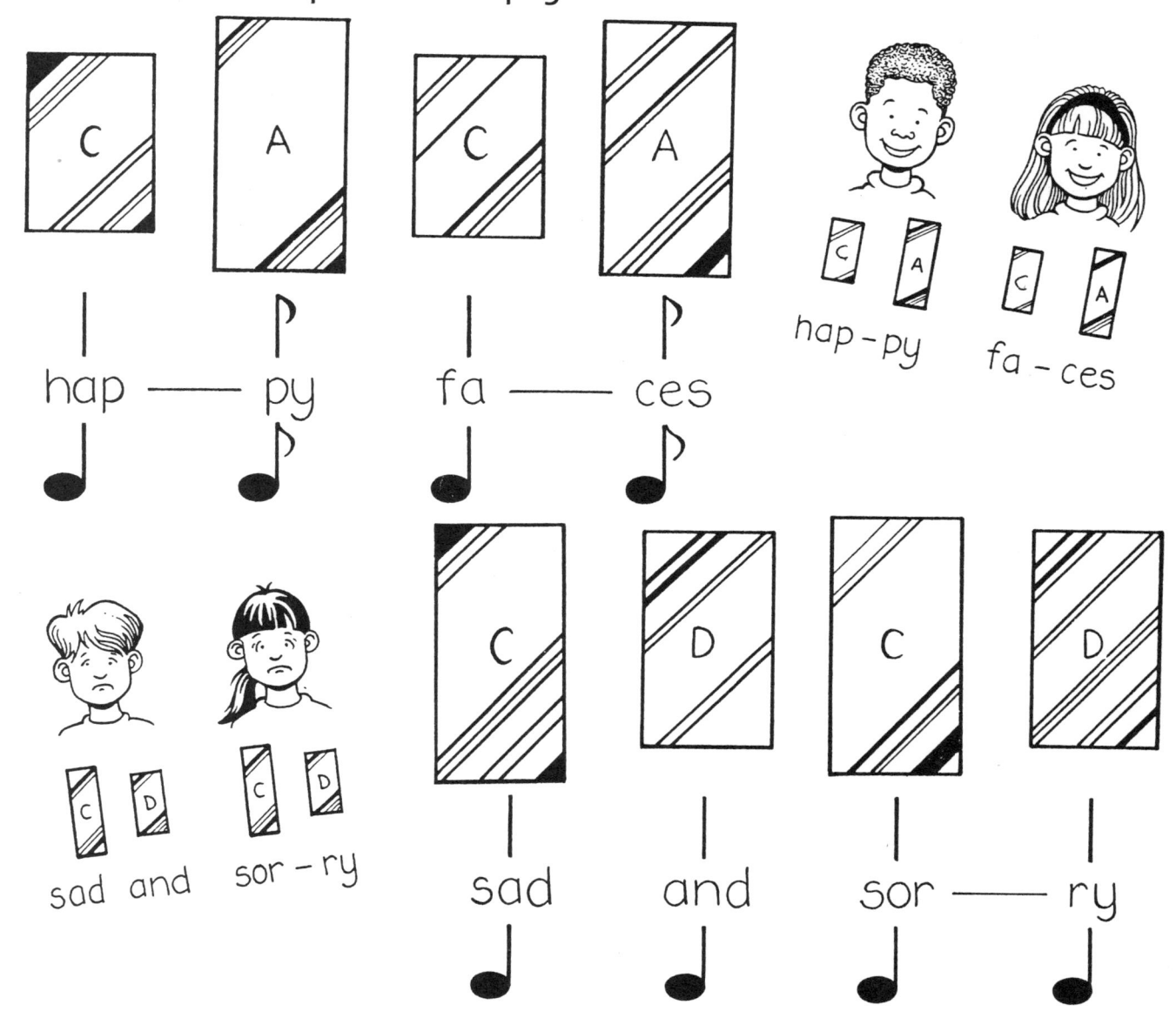

C	A		C	A
hap — py			fa — ces	

hap-py   fa-ces

sad and sor-ry

C	D	C	D
sad	and	sor — ry	

© Folens (copiable page)   IDEAS BANK – *Songs and Rhymes*

Old and new – Ideas page

Key idea

- To introduce more songs and rhymes to use for composition and performance.

Starting points

- Read the two songs below about pancakes. Is one of the songs older than the other? How can the children tell? (The second rhyme, *But hark*, uses old fashioned language).
- Explain that they will need to make this rhyme sound older than the first one. How will they do this? This is difficult. For example, they could use a bell sound and toll it at the beginning and the end of the rhyme.

Mix a pancake,
Stir a pancake,
Pop it in the pan.
Fry the pancake,
Toss the pancake,
Catch it if you can.

(Traditional)

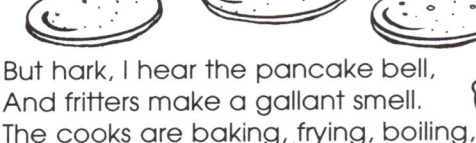

But hark, I hear the pancake bell,
And fritters make a gallant smell.
The cooks are baking, frying, boiling,
Stewing, mincing, roasting, toasting.

(Adapted from *Poor Robin's Almanac*, 1684)

Activities

- Read this poem from *Pillow Talk* by Roger McGough (Viking, 1990). Ask the children to make a tune for it.
- Divide the class into five groups and give each one a different verse. Then join the five different tunes together to make a complete song.
- Alternatively the children could create sound effects for each verse. Divide the words among narrators.
- Give the children a copy of the rhythm bank on the activity page. It contains ideas that will help them to read and write musical notation for their tune. Block out any sections not needed.
- They may want to write out some music for their tune. Ask them to show their musical scores or pictures to another teacher or group. The music or the pictures should indicate to them how the song will go.

The all-purpose children's poem

The first verse contains a princess,
two witches (one evil, one Good)
There is a castle in it somewhere
And a dark and tangled wood.

The second has ghosts and vampires,
Monsters with foul-smelling breath.
It sends shivers down the book spine
And scares everybody to death.

The third is one of my favourites
With rabbits in skirts and trousers
Who talk to each other like we do
And live in neat little houses.

The fourth verse is bang up to date
And in it anything goes.
Set in the city, it doesn't rhyme
(Although, in a way, it does).

The fifth is set in the future
(And as you can see, it's the last)
When the Word was made Computer
And books are a thing of the past.

2030 AD

IDEAS BANK – *Songs and Rhymes*

Rhythm bank

- Use these ideas to help make your own tune.

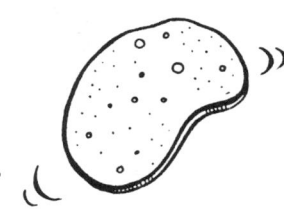

bak—ing fry—ing

Mix	a	pan—cake	
✗	✗	✗	✗
stir	a	pan—cake	
✗	✗	✗	✗
pop	it	in	a
✗	✗	✗	✗
pan			
✗	—	—	—

Skip—ping quick—ly

G   E   G   E

Rab-bits in | Skirts and | trou-sers

Musical glossary

Accompaniment	– a background for a solo or main tune.
Beat	– a regular pulse in a piece of music.
Crescendo	– getting louder.
Crotchet	– a one-beat note written as ♩ 2/4 means two crochet beats in a bar. 3/4 means three crochet beats in a bar.
Decrescendo	– (or Diminuendo) getting softer.
Dynamics	– different levels of volume, for instance, loud, getting louder or soft.
Graphic score	– a written piece of music that uses symbols instead of standard notation.
Minim	– a two-beat note written as ♩
Ostinato	– a short repeated pattern of sounds or notes, for instance, 'clap–stamp, clap–stamp' or 'C–G, C–G, C–G' used as an accompaniment.
Percussion	– any instrument whose sound is produced by striking or shaking.
Pitch	– the location of a sound as high or low.
Pulse	– the repeating, steady beat that can be felt in most music.
Rhythm	– the beat or pulse of music.
Structure	– the 'shape' or plan of music, for example, a piece in three sections (A B A).
Tempo	– the speed or pace of music, for instance, fast or slow.
Texture	– the way in which sounds are put together, for example, melody and accompaniment.
Timbre	– the quality (tone colour) of sound, for example, harsh or smooth. Each sound source has its own distinctive timbre.
Tonic solfa	– a pitch ladder that goes 'doh, ray, me, fah, soh, lah, te, doh'.
Verse	– a repeated tune with varying words.

IDEAS BANK – *Songs and Rhymes* © Folens (copiable page)